LEO XIV: THE NEW POPE AND CATHOLIC REFORM

LEO XIV: THE NEW POPE AND CATHOLIC REFORM

by
Christopher R. Altieri

CONTINUUM RELIGION

BLOOMSBURY CONTINUUM
Bloomsbury Publishing Plc
50 Bedford Square, London, WC1B 3DP, UK
Bloomsbury Publishing Ireland Limited
29 Earlsfort Terrace, Dublin 2, D02 AY28, Ireland

First published in Great Britain 2025

Photos © ANDREJ ISAKOVIC/AFP via Getty Images; Vatican Media/Vatican Pool – Corbis/
Getty Images; Mario Tomassetti – Vatican Media via Vatican Pool/Getty Images; Stefano
Costantino/SOPA Images/LightRocket via Getty Images; Simone Risoluti – Vatican Media via
Vatican Pool/Getty Images; Francesco Sforza – Vatican Media via Vatican Pool/Getty Images;
Massimo Valicchia/NurPhoto via Getty Images; Massimo Valicchia/NurPhoto via Getty Images;
Grzegorz Galazka/Archivio Grzegorz Galazka/Mondadori Portfolio via Getty Images; Fiorani
Fabio/Alamy; Riccardo De Luca/Anadolu via Getty Images; Elisabetta Trevisan – Vatican Media
via Vatican Pool/Getty Images; AFP PHOTO/CHICLAYO DIOSECE; Simone Risoluti –
Vatican Media via Vatican Pool/Getty Images; marco iacobucci/SOPA Images/LightRocket via
Getty Images; TIZIANA FABI/AFP via Getty Images

A catalogue record for this book is available from the British Library

Library of Congress Cataloguing-in-Publication data has been applied for

ISBN: HB: 978-1-3994-3089-0; TPB: 978-1-3994-3088-3; eBook: 978-1-3994-3090-6;
ePDF: 978-1-3994-3084-5

2 4 6 8 10 9 7 5 3 1

Typeset by Lumina Datamatics Ltd
Printed and bound in Great Britain by Clays Ltd, Elcograf S.p.A

For Charley

Contents

Preface and acknowledgments

The election of Leo XIV, a son of Saint Augustine, is a momentous event in the life of the Church and of the world. This book is meant only to offer just a very little in the way of introduction to the man who has come into the papal office and to offer a view of the office into which Leo has come, perhaps under a new and different light. I have tried to write of the papacy itself, as much as I have endeavoured to write of Leo, and of the Catholic Church in the world of what is fast becoming the middle of the twenty-first century. I have drawn on my experience—nearly a quarter-century in Rome—and on what learning I could bring to bear on a subject that vastly outstrips any one writer. The book looks backward and forward, sometimes in turns and sometimes at once, but I hope to have captured the sense of focused calm about the business that—startling to me—accompanied its writing. I have written this book speedily, nevertheless, and very much in response to events that were sudden even if they were not unexpected.

To what my efforts have come is now yours to decide and to tell, but they would have come to nothing without the help of too many people even to mention. Friends, in particular, Josh Mansfield, Gregory Di Pippo, Robert Krishna OP, Nicolas Steeves SJ, Carl E. Olson, Robert P. George, Amy Welborn, Stephen Bullivant, John L. Allen Jr., Elise Ann Allen, Francis X. Rocca, Deirdre Brennan, Sam Kachuba, and many others I will not mention in order not to condition their public engagement with the book before you, all helped in various ways deserving of special mention. You will see that I have relied on the work of a great many journalists beside those mentioned in these acknowledgments, many of them friends of many years as well as colleagues in the profession. My thanks to them and to all who work or have worked the old beat.

My editor, Dominic Mattos, shepherded the project with astounding patience and quiet confidence, gently and expertly taking an inchoate vision of what could be, through a very compressed schedule of drafting and revision. Every one of his suggestions made the book better. I could not have done this without him. Sarah Jones did utterly astounding work as project editor, under excruciating time constraints. She turned a complex manuscript into a beautifully prepared book, with supreme intelligence and admirable aplomb. My thanks to her and to the whole production team at Bloomsbury.

Hugh Allan O. Praem. introduced me to Dominic, and for that I shall be forever grateful. Christopher Wells was a sounding board, and more, throughout this project, for which I am grateful. Stephen White and Philip Larrey gave generously of their time and expertise to help me better understand technical points in their fields, for which I am likewise grateful.

My son, Joseph, read an early draft of the manuscript and offered enormously helpful criticism, cheerfully and wittily lighting the path and deftly showing how to smooth what were some very rough patches. My wife, Ester, consulted with me at great length on several points of canon law, history, and language. My daughter, Rachel, cheerfully and gamely kept me in coffee, seltzer water, and snacks, picked up slack in the garden, and did a thousand other like services, without which the issue should have been very much in doubt.

Everything good in this book is theirs. Any mistakes or infelicities are entirely my own.

Christopher R. Altieri
Fairfield, CT, 30 July 2025

Chapter 1

A radical choice

"It's going to be Zuppi," I said to a fellow—a parish priest and a family friend of many years—no more than a few days before the cardinals went into conclave. "He'll be elected on the second ballot of the afternoon on the third day," I said, "and he'll take the name, Innocent," my tone carrying an air of confidence that flirted with *suffisance*. Matteo Cardinal Zuppi was the Archbishop of Bologna and the president of the *Conferenza Episcopale Italiana*—the Italian bishops' national conference—meaning he had experience in pastoral government and complex administrative leadership. He was close to Rome and understood Roman ways, but was not a Roman curial lifer. He had experience as a special diplomatic envoy but had not made a career of diplomatic service. He was a theological moderate friendly to people and tolerant of groups across the spectrum of opinion in the Church. Zuppi, at last, was a known quantity to the scores of cardinal-electors with little depth-knowledge of Rome or each other. I am glad I did not have money on Zuppi's name.

The cardinal protodeacon, Dominique Mamberti, came to the loggia above St. Peter's Basilica on 8th May, 2025, and intoned words at once mystical and familiar: *Annuntio vobis Gaudium magnum: Habemus papam! Eminentissimum ac reverendissimum dominum, dominum Robertum Franciscum, Sanctae Romanae Ecclesiae cardinalem Prevost, qui sibi nomen imposuit Leonem decimum quartum!* I was live to air on LNL, a DC-based service that covers breaking news and events for local markets throughout the US, and I remember the moment when I realized what had happened: "Robert ...*Francis?*" I thought, "that's Prevost!" In my head, I pronounced his surname with the stress on the first syllable: *PREE*-vost. Mamberti, it seemed to me, pronounced a short—or an open—first syllable and stressed rather the second syllable, roughly: Pray-*VOST*. By the time that titbit registered, however, I was already scrambling to pull together a few biographical details in my head. If memory serves, the producer cut away from me for a brief spell while Cardinal Mamberti announced Leo and I said, "I know who he is," though I'm not sure for whom I said it.

In fairness to me, the Vatican watchers who had Robert Francis Cardinal Prevost OSA as even a remote possibility were relatively few. The chief reason for which this transplanted Yankee thought Prevost too unlikely to consider, was that Prevost came from the US, too. According to the conventional wisdom, no fellow from the US really stood any chance. Giving the papacy to someone from the US would tie the "soft power" of the papal office to the "hard power" of US geopolitical and cultural clout. Nobody wanted that, I surmised, correctly but incompletely. The quarter century this scribbler spent in the Eternal City (most of that time covering the pope and the Vatican in one way or another) ought to have brought a series of considerations to the fore and into focus, beginning with the fact that Prevost was a transplant, as well.

The man we now call Pope Leo XIV had lived most of his life outside his native United States, and most of that time far from his native home he had spent in service as a missionary priest and later bishop in Peru, or in Rome as the head of his religious order. He had filled other senior leadership roles in the Order of Saint Augustine, before his two terms as prior general of the OSAs in Rome from 2001–13. He had completed advanced studies in canon law at Rome's Pontifical University of St. Thomas Aquinas (the Dominican university commonly known as the Angelicum in honour of its patron and namesake, the *Doctor Angelicus* or "Angelic Doctor") and served again in Rome from 2023 until his election, as prefect of the Roman curial department responsible—among other things—for vetting episcopal candidates. Conversations—mine and others'—with people who had spent time in the pre-conclave meetings and around the conclave that elected Prevost confirm that all those specific details of biography played a significant part in the cardinals' discernment.

Leo XIV, in short, is a man of three worlds: born in the second city of the most powerful nation in history; tempered and seasoned in the impoverished global south; familiar with the Eternal City that is the seat of global Catholicism's supreme power and home to the Church's central governing apparatus. In the few minutes I had between the live announcement of Prevost's election and a one-on-one with Ryan Piers of LNL, I was able to pull together something serviceable. I turned my initial thoughts into a short piece for *Crux* that ran on Sunday, May 11th, and put a little—but only a little—flesh on the bones I had assembled live-to-air.

Profile of a pope

While I was talking live-to-air and then while I was drafting the piece for *Crux*, I began to realize how well Prevost—now Leo XIV—fit the profile of the fellow for which I was sure the cardinals would be looking. He fit the bill much better than did even Zuppi—the fellow I thought the red hats would choose—and indeed better than anyone else in the college I could call to mind. The profile I had sketched for myself and for readers in the days before the conclave was of a man who would be a steady pair of hands:

- He would be an institutionalist by character and temperament. He would know how the machinery of Roman government was supposed to work, but he would not be a cog in the Roman machine.

- He would have a real sense of the Church's place in the international community and a real appreciation of the Church's role in the international order, but he would not be a career diplomat.
- He would understand from the inside out, the Church's global footprint and cultural purpose in all its myriad local varieties and incarnations, but he would not be a "culture-warrior" or a partisan.
- He would have experience in pastoral government and demonstrated pastoral sensibility, but he would not tend to view the responsible administration of pastoral solicitude—what Catholics call "care of souls" in their peculiar technical parlance—as work necessarily opposed to law, custom, morality, or tradition in both the broad and the narrow senses in which Catholics use the term.

The reasons for which I expected the cardinals to be looking for someone fitting that profile were complex and multifarious but boiled down to three broadly converging considerations. I will have more to say about each of them during the course of this book, but here and now and in brief, they were: exhaustion at the end of a twelve-year whirlwind pontificate; global sociopolitical and economic disruption; Vatican insolvency and general dysfunction.

First, the pontificate of Francis had been exhausting. Pope Francis' dozen-year reign was one of contradictions. Francis preached something he called "synodality" and apparently intended as a broadly consultative approach to government, but he governed autocratically and arguably concentrated more power in the person of the Roman pontiff than had any pope since the time of the Reformation. Francis would say one thing and do another—one thinks of his repeated "No" to ordaining women to the diaconate as currently constituted, often uttered either before or after naming a commission to study the question—and he occasionally said both things and did a third. *Hagan lio!* was his rallying cry to young people (which one could render generously as, "Stir things up!" but it more closely translates to, "Make a mess!") and it is fair to say he led by example. Even people broadly sympathetic to his person and in step with his agenda for the Church, such as it was, were ready for some regularity in government when the time came for new leadership.

Second, the world in May of the year 2025 was very much changed since 2013 and was changing before everyone's eyes, even the occasionally myopic eyes of the Church's princes. Trends already discernible when Francis came to power were well advanced, such as religious disaffiliation in Europe and the United States and defection from Catholicism in Latin America, the rise of China as a global superpower, and the explosive growth of African and Asian Christianity—especially Catholicism—which had already begun to shift the Church's "centre of gravity" from the global north and west to the global south and east. Social media had already begun to make the world smaller and meaner—and to exert a baleful influence on discourse both in the Church and in society—while the rise of artificial intelligence was presenting new challenges and opportunities in 2025, which had been only dimly on the horizon in 2013. Rare earth minerals—key raw materials for the technologies both established and emerging in the digital age—had joined fossil fuels as drivers of strategic political, economic, and military interest. Whether one considers geopolitical shifts, technological developments, economic, financial, and commercial realignments and rearrangements, demographic sea changes, cultural fluctuations and disruptions, the general appearance and feeling was that the project of global civilization was very much the opposite of stable (and quite possibly teetering).

Third, the challenges facing the Vatican were—are—daunting. The cardinals were aware of a burgeoning financial crisis in the Vatican, the pinch of which they had long since begun to feel both personally and officially, especially the cardinals with curial billets. Several major scandals of abuse and cover-up, some of them reaching the very highest echelons of ecclesiastical power and a few of them even touching Francis personally, had revealed an ecclesiastical justice system and leadership culture both in grave disarray. The Catholic Church's entire central governing apparatus was dysfunctional (not to say sclerotic) on a good day. Those are only three of the major issues facing the highest levels of government in the Church.

The cardinals who would elect the successor to Pope Francis had all that in mind when they went into the Sistine Chapel. They were also sensible of another fact, central and ineluctable, of the contemporary papacy: In the twenty-first century—really since the reign of Pope St. John Paul II—the papal office had become spectacular. That development meant the cardinals would be looking for someone who could carry an audience, someone with stage presence and command of at least a few major world languages sufficient to engage and hold both individual interlocutors and a large public gathering.

Pope St. John Paul II, for all his prodigious strengths, was mostly content to delegate the day-to-day work of government to the Curia while he trotted the globe, galvanizing crowds in historic numbers wherever he went. Benedict XVI did well enough in public and sometimes extraordinarily well, but was by his own admission a weak administrator who governed little when he governed at all. Pope Francis, elected with a mandate to reform the Church's central governing apparatus, undertook a project even more ambitious than curial reform; he barely completed a paper overhaul of the central government and in any case governed largely without his Curia. All this meant the cardinals were looking for someone resistant to the allure of the limelight who also would not wither under it, and would be willing to stay at home and govern the Church.

At one point in the run-up to the conclave, I mused in the *Catholic World Report*[1] about how the profile I had sketched did remind me of Meredith Willson's *The Music Man*, and more particularly of an exchange between the heroine of that delightful musical and her Irish-American mother, who reproved her daughter's erstwhile spurning of the story's ne'er-do-well protagonist, "Prof." Harold Hill. Marian Paroo (the heroine) describes Hill as a "common masher" and protests that she has her "standards" when it comes to the men she would allow to vie for her affections. "[I]f you don't mind my sayin' so," Mrs. Paroo offers by way of rejoinder (she very nearly interrupts her daughter), "there's not a man alive who could hope to measure up to that blend of Paul Bunyan, Saint Pat, and Noah Webster you've concocted for yourself out of your Irish imagination, your Iowa stubbornness, and your li'berry full of books!" The cardinals, in other words, were looking for an institutionalist who would not be afraid to use a firm hand when and where one is needed; a governor with the pastoral touch and a diplomat's care with words; a fellow who understands global politics and has a global perspective but is not a career diplomat; a man with senior administrative leadership experience who is not a career bureaucrat. Any one of those would have been a tall order.

The cardinals were also remarkably clear-eyed in one other respect. They knew that Francis' successor would not have much in the way of a honeymoon with the press. Francis had been tremendous for reporters right from the start. He curated the media narrative around him and his pontificate meticulously. The scribbling and chattering classes mostly bought into the narrative Francis fostered. By the time reporters began to notice the warts, as it were, it was too late for the stories of misrule engendered by his reign to receive the attention they deserved or make much lasting impact on public perception of the pope or his pontificate.

The cardinals knew that *Vaticanisti*—as the reporters who cover the pope and the Vatican are called in Italian—were unlikely to let their editors become invested in any such narrative, were one even proffered this time. There was unfinished business from the Francis pontificate, as well, requiring urgent address. Resisting pressure to act precipitously, while also avoiding too much delay, was going to be a challenge for the new pope. It was going to be a challenge even without media pressure, and there was going to be media pressure, almost from Day One. The cardinals could not hope for more than a fair shake from the press for the man they would choose.

Pope Leo: What happened?

All that was racing through my head, inchoate, as I processed the news of Leo's election in real time. When one colleague asked me whether I thought the new pope would continue in Pope Francis' progressive agenda for the Church, I remember challenging the premise in my reply, saying roughly that the narrative of Francis-as-progressive never seemed to me to fit very well. I understood well how Francis had earned the reputation he had. He frequently spoke and behaved like a parish priest—often to powerful and even bracing effect—but the universal Church is not a global parish (or a global province of the Jesuit order to which Francis belonged). The papal office is one of government, and the cardinals were going to choose a man who would govern in a manner very different from that of Francis. They had gone into conclave looking for a different sort of governor and they emerged having chosen Prevost as Pope Leo XIV.

You will likely recall your grade school lessons about what we call the "Five Ws" in the trade: *Who? What? Where? When? Why?* I recall how I was flummoxed for a second or two—it felt like an eternity—as I tried to organize the things I knew for sure about the man I now needed to know as Leo and present them as helpfully as I could to a public only marginally less prepared than I. So, my journalistic instincts took over and took me through the Five Ws.

That last W—*Why?*—is the one that most often appears to be the most difficult. *Why?* is a synthesis of the first four Ws. It is always hard to nail down even one *Why?* and the situations in which there is only one of them, well, to call them "vanishingly rare" would be gross understatement. *Why?* also has—or may have—multiple objects: "Why did this happen?" is one question; "Why ought one care?" is another (and a very different kind of question). *Why?* is also—and therefore—often the most difficult to articulate, even when one has a handle on the substance of an answer to it.

There are myriad wrong answers to any *Why?* question. There are myriad right ways of thinking about *Why?* questions in general and about what I would like to call *Why?*-adjacent questions, as well. There are myriad wrong ways of thinking about *Why?* questions, too, but there is no answer to any of them as is or may be simply right. *Why?* however, is not the fundamental question. The fundamental question is: *What?* With Prevost's election to the See of St. Peter, the *What?* and the *Who?* coincided in a way that I knew would take a good deal of unpacking. That is, in short, the story of the genesis of this book, the purpose of which is not only or even primarily to chart a way toward answers to as many of the fundamental questions as may prove possible in the short space of it, but to survey and map out the world into which Pope Leo XIV has come as the leader of global Catholicism in the middle of the twenty-first century.

The Challenge of Reform

The Church is in need of reform and the world is in need of the Church. She is present in the developed and in the developing world through her work in areas like healthcare, education, child and elder care, and other Catholic social services from athletics to scouting, arts, and culture more generally. The organizations that do such and similar work are happy to make converts, in the main, but their purpose is not to proselytise. They are about their business primarily because their faith compels them to work for the upbuilding of human personality and society. They sometimes describe themselves as "apostolates of presence" in the Catholic parlance. Even from a merely sociological point-of-view, the Catholic Church plays an important role in every society to which she is present, and she is present just about everywhere.

You may not notice her quietly about her work, frequently through shoestring initiatives of the faithful who operate without support from the bishops—and occasionally in the face of some interference or resistance from hierarchical leadership—and through her many local and international outreach organizations. If the Church were to cease her help to the poor, the young, the old, the weak, the sick, and the vulnerable, you would notice her absence in very short order. The Church plays a role in politics and public moral debate, not only by raising her voice directly, but by forming so many people from elementary school to university. Catholic educational apostolates do much to form political and cultural leadership classes even in countries where Catholics are a tiny minority. Catholic schools, in the main, do not seek to make converts of their pupils or students. They form boys and girls, adolescents, and young men and women for responsible citizenship. There are lots of places on this planet where Catholic school is the only educational option, especially for girls and young women.

The Catholic Church matters, in short, and that is why she needs to put herself in form for twenty-first-century action. I am not talking about revisiting settled matters of Church teaching or even about the ways in which the Church couches and presents to the world her understanding of life, the universe, and everything. Doctrinal unsettlement—or the appearance of it, at any rate—was one of the hallmarks of the Francis pontificate. People across the spectrum of opinion in the Church, leaders and faithful alike, would rather be past it. Church teaching has a way of sorting itself out, in any case. Problems of government—problems arising from power and its organization, in other words—generally do not sort themselves.

There is an old saying that has become something of a maxim in leadership circles: "Amateurs talk strategy, professionals talk logistics." It is a saying often attributed (erroneously, most likely) to the WWII-era US Gen. Omar N. Bradley. The statement aptly expresses the idea that leaders always do well to focus on facts; to develop a clear-eyed view of the facts as completely as practicable, with a view to developing and executing a plan rooted in what is really feasible rather than a grand vision of an ideal state.[2] Applied to the Church, one could say: "Amateurs talk doctrine; professionals talk governance."

That is the sense in which I will be speaking of Church reform in this book. Like it or not, the Church is a power structure. If that is too reductive—one may fairly urge that the Church is not merely a power structure—even a lifelong coenobite mystic must admit that the Church has a power structure and indeed a divinely given hierarchical constitution. More to the point, any sophomore student of history will know that the ways in which the Church organizes power and exercises it have changed through the years and centuries of her pilgrim life on Earth.

There is a very real sense in which the Church is always in need of reform: *Ecclesia semper reformanda* is the Latin phrase some Catholics use to express the idea. One way I have tried to describe the notion is by comparison of the Church to an old machine, charmingly antique and in many ways implausibly reliable. One may find in an artisan's laboratory even today, or occasionally see one on the road and about trade. The artisan or tradesman needs his machine to be in working order, and that is a proposition both costly and labour-intensive.

The fellow would gladly give the old clunker to a mechanic (or a machinist expert with antiques), but has no substitute and cannot replace it. It is almost certain that a sufficiently knowledgeable and resourceful pair of hands could, given several months or even a few weeks to tinker with the contraption, discover which parts need replacing and which refurbishing. There are such hands about, but the artisan needs the machine to fill an order today—and every day—so cannot afford to have it offline for any protracted length of time. The best the artisan or tradesman can do—who knows his own machine, inside and out, better than any hired help—is to keep it running for a few hours at a stretch.

To use a nautical simile—one that fits well with a society that calls itself the "barque of St. Peter"—the Church is like a ship, the crew of which must make repairs underway. The captain may dispose what he will, but there are real practical limits to what even the most clever, seasoned, and resourceful complement of sailors can do while she is at sea. When it comes to Church reform, in other words, there is a practically achievable good that will always be closer to "good enough" than it may ever come to anything perfect or even very much better. That's not to say that real reform is impossible, but it is to say a great deal about what successful reform looks like, and successful reform of Church structures and Church leadership culture has happened before.

What reform looks like

My go-to example of successful Church reform in the sense I have outlined above is from the Council of Trent (1545–63). Trent was the longest Council in the history of the Church, and it was a long time coming. Before Trent, there had been several desultory attempts to change this or that, none of them terribly well considered or anything close to wholehearted. Trent was finally summoned in response to the burgeoning crisis of what Catholics at the time called "the Lutheran schism" that was tearing the whole society of Christians in the West to pieces and threatening to tear the Holy Roman Empire apart.

Trent was a mixed bag, but among its more successful reforms was one that required bishops to reside within the geographical confines of the jurisdictions they govern. If the Catholic bishop of your diocese lives within a postal code or two of you—and, chances are, he does—you have the Council of Trent and its successful implementation to thank for it. For hundreds of years before Trent, however, bishops frequently did not live within their nominal jurisdictions. Local Churches were sees-in-gift, not entirely unlike fiefs to a monarch, which crowned heads would use to make political arrangements.

Sometimes, kings and emperors and popes (who were a little of both the former in those days) would placate rivals by giving them a bishopric and the tax revenue that came with it. They often did not much care whether the new man ever stepped foot within his new jurisdiction (and sometimes rather preferred he did not). On other occasions, they would be forming or shoring up alliances. Occasionally, they were only looking after family. As happened in the case of Henry II and Thomas Becket, monarchs were now and again inclined to see that they had a friendly fellow in a powerful position. Whatever were or may have been rulers' reasons for behaving as they did, their behaviour in such and similar regards was a chief complaint among the reform-minded.

The bishops who participated in the Council of Trent, with the help of theologians and experts in Church law (called "canonists" for their knowledge and practice in the body of ecclesiastical legislation and jurisprudence called canon law), imposed a residency requirement on bishops. Getting the law on paper was a big step, but it was only the beginning of a cultural change. More than a century would pass before one could say that bishops residing in their jurisdictions was the norm in fact as well as law. There are bishops who wander more than perhaps they ought even today, in the rough present of the twenty-first century.

In an address delivered on 19 September 2013 to recently consecrated bishops who were in Rome for a crash course on the ins and outs of episcopal life, Pope Francis decried the "scandal of being 'airport bishops'," by which he meant the bad example given by the sort who are always jetting off to Rome or somewhere else, instead of staying home and governing. "[R]esidence is not only required for the purpose of good organization," Francis said, "it has a theological root," which he not only asserted but elaborated. "You are bridegrooms of your community," Francis said, "deeply bound to [them]." He urged the "baby bishops" to "remain among [their] people." If, in 2013, the pope was still feeling the need to remind bishops of their duty to live with their people, it is fair to say the problem has proved rather persistent. What has changed is not only that airport bishops are by now rather the exception than the rule, but that the default and expected thing is for bishops really to live within the confines of the dioceses they govern.

That, in short, is what reform looks like: a temporary and imperfect admixture of paper legal reform prudently crafted, diligently applied over years and decades and even centuries until cultural defaults have not only shifted but settled into a new and at least (sometimes at most) marginally better place. Reform is a lengthy process. Reform is a cumbersome affair. Reform requires decisive action at crucial moments. Reform requires patience, diligence, and vigilance. Reform is always incomplete.

Anyone pining for ages past, as though there were an epoch d'or to which Catholics (or any of us) could return, will find no such era recorded in history. Even the *Acts of the Apostles*—that's the book of the New Testament in which the exploits of the earliest Christians are recorded—tells all-too-human stories of cowardice, imprudence, dishonesty, haste and rashness, almost every weakness to which flesh is heir, with occasional flashes of genius and punctuated by feats of superhuman and indeed supernatural virtue. The great story in *Acts*—the overarching story or the story of the stories, if you will—is indeed one of unlikely success or even *eucatastrophe*, to say it with J.R.R. Tolkien, in which God is always at work.

Pope Leo XIV himself said as much on the Solemnity of Saints Peter and Paul—29 June 2025—in his *Angelus* remarks. "The New Testament does not conceal the errors, conflicts and sins of those whom we venerate as the greatest Apostles," Leo said, in remarks to the faithful gathered in St Peter's Square under the Roman sky at noon to recite the ancient prayer of

Marian devotion. "Their greatness was shaped by forgiveness," Leo also said. "The risen Lord reached out to them more than once," Leo continued, "to put them back on the right path. Jesus never calls just one time. That is why we can always hope." Anyone who reads the *Acts* and comes away believing it to be a vademecum on good government has missed the point.

Nor is there a golden age on the horizon. Catholics believe and confess the Church triumphant, indeed, but the fullness of her triumph is to come in the celestial Jerusalem that is beyond history. While we are in time, we mostly muddle. The work of reform, therefore, is ever-needful and mostly of the muddling sort.[3] The Church will never make an end of reform, because she will never but hardly begin it and cannot put in for overhaul. The Church, in short, is like the tradesman at pains to keep his truck in some sort of repair, and even more like the captain ordering repairs while the vessel under his command is underway.

"A muddy business"

Two other images, both from ages past and both of late returned to vogue in some Catholic circles, may also help to bring the business into focus: *Ecclesia militans* and *Ecclesia peregrinans*, the "Church Militant" and the "Pilgrim Church". These days, saying "Church Militant" often evokes images of knights in brilliant armour and bright soldiers, spears bristling under colours unfurled and dancing in the wind. Sometimes, people speaking of the Church Militant have in mind what C.S. Lewis's fictional demon, Screwtape, called, "[T]he Church as we see her, spread out through all time and space and rooted in eternity, terrible as an army with banners." When we think or speak of the Pilgrim Church, we likewise often think of merry days on sunlit paths well marked and peopled with fellows, of song and wine and the sure promise of shelter and a hot meal at the end of every stretch. While there may be more than a little truth to the former and the latter image, the workaday realities of the soldier's as well as the pilgrim's life are rather grimy.

Soldiering is muddy business, as is the business of peregrination. Soldiers and pilgrims were until very recently not likely to make a natural end to life, and the former are still very much less likely than the latter or than any of us, to die in bed after a long life. Hunger, disease, exposure, or workaday violence were far more probable for both than battle and old age. In the main, military camps and pilgrim ways and hostels are today more regular and sanitary than ever before in history, but the world is not wanting for bandits and murderers. There will be such characters among us until the end of time.

Catholics are right to expect that their leaders be protectors rather than thieves or worse, to demand that their rulers in the faith not put themselves in league with such or similar. Catholics have a right, therefore, to knowledge of their rulers' conduct and character even and especially when the men who should be their shepherds are reckless, negligent, wicked, or stupid. Roughly as I put it in an article for *Catholic Answers*[4] a few years back, in which I first teased the ideas I have been sketching here, Catholics have a right to clean and orderly camps, as well as to hostels (or "hospitals") competently staffed and regularly operated.

The world is dangerous. No one escapes it alive. Awareness of the fact keeps Catholics vigilant as well as others, or ought to do at any rate. That ineluctable fact is also precisely why Catholics have always considered themselves on the march, on the move, on the way. It also expresses the commitment of Catholics to serving their fellows in humanity. *Milito, militare,* from which we get words like militant and military, is a verb denoting a very specific form of service, with manifold possibilities in the world under the standard of the Cross and also with some definite—and definitely inconvenient—limitations. All this ought to bring both the possibilities and the limits of reform sharply into focus.

A book about the possibilities and limits of reform under Pope Leo XIV cannot fail, therefore, to mention and indeed to discuss at some length the state of the Church, into the supreme government of which Leo has come. Any such discussion must in turn involve an unsparing look at the pontificate of Leo's predecessor. This presents significant challenges to both the author and the reader. The book cannot become a mere critical examination primarily of what has been, but it must not leave a reader without contextual wherewithal to understand the present.

Throughout his pontificate, from his unassuming *Buona sera!* spoken to the faithful from the loggia above St. Peter's Basilica to his, *Grazie per avermi portato in piazza*—"Thank you for bringing me to the square"—given to his nurse on Easter Sunday of 2025 and reportedly the last words he spoke on Earth, Pope Francis hid himself in plain sight. He was a man who contained multitudes, always at once veiling and disclosing himself. His life and times—his person as well as his reign—deserve patient and careful treatment, but that is the work of another and a very different book.

The life of Pope Leo XIV is equally deserving of such patient and careful treatment, which nevertheless cannot be the subject of this book either. As I have come to conceive of it, this book is in one respect biography-adjacent. It points toward the need for a full biography of Leo XIV. Its main usefulness, however, is in its capture of the sweep and scope of history—especially, though not exclusively, recent history—bringing into hard focus the real circumstances of the Church Leo XIV must govern and the world in which he must govern her.

All throughout the whole of a career that now spans three decades and four pontificates, I have been chiefly concerned with the pope as supreme governor of the Church. Others have done excellent work chronicling, profiling, investigating, explaining, and arguing out papal teaching. Journalism as I care about it most deeply is the practice of vigilance. The watchdog function of the fourth estate is primary and indispensable. I have always endeavoured to conduct my practice of the profession so as to make candid my commitment to that understanding.

I have acquitted myself, I believe, tolerably well in that regard. Whether I have really succeeded, here or ever, is beyond my power to tell.

The papacy is an impossible burden. That is why Catholics pray for the pope—whoever he is—and it is why no one in his right mind should ever desire to succeed St. Peter in his See of Rome. If no one in his right mind would desire the papacy, the thought of refusing it once it has been offered—or of giving it up once one has accepted it—should terrify any sane man. History will judge how well or poorly any man has discharged the duties of papal office, but history neither happens in a vacuum nor does it write itself, and history's first draft is journalism. Only God may judge the soul of any man who has sat on Peter's throne, and Catholics confidently hope God shall judge mercifully anyone who gives sincere and wholehearted service by what light is given him to see and serve in that dreadful siege.

Who is the man now in the office and with what must he contend on the stage that is the world, as it turns into the middle of the twenty-first century, before the ruthless eyes of history and on his way to eternity?

Chapter 2

A restless heart

The story of Robert Francis Prevost is at once commonplace and fascinating, even uncanny, precisely because it is so very much the story of a mid-century boy of the Midwestern United States, born into a middle-class family that lived in the middle of a postwar suburban development. The times of the Prevost family in Robert's generation were heady indeed. There was explosive economic growth, and also social unrest as intolerable racial divisions began finally to sear the national conscience after centuries of lacerating the nation in body and soul. Around the world, Europe was experiencing the Cold War— think of the Soviet suppression of the Hungarian Revolution in 1956 and the Prague Spring of 1968—while peoples and political societies throughout the global south were agitating for independence from their erstwhile European colonial rulers. Catholic culture in the United States was approaching its zenith, driven in part by the baby boom and in part by the prosperity the second, third, and fourth generations of Catholic immigrants were achieving.

The world was restless—nothing new—but getting at once smaller and very much larger. The space race was expanding the horizon of human endeavour, while the arms race was making the spectre of global nuclear annihilation to loom large on it. Morals were shifting in ways that made it appear as if nothing were stable, even as though there were no truth abiding. It was an age increasingly in need of hearing Saint Augustine's sublime encapsulation of the human condition: "You made us unto yourself, and until it should rest in you, our heart is restless."[5] It was an age increasingly incapable of hearing it.

Rob, as his friends and family knew him in his boyhood, experienced the restlessness of his human heart before he had words with which to describe it or a spiritual patrimony by which to direct it. In the experience of restlessness, he is like every one of us. His story is one that sets in relief what the late Harvard philosopher and film critic, Stanley Cavell (1926–2018), liked to call, "the uncanniness of the ordinary," by which he meant, "the sense of the human as inherently strange, say unstable, its quotidian as forever fantastic."[6] It bears mention that Cavell was about the preparation and delivery of those lectures while the Chicago man who would become Pope Leo XIV was at work on a research doctorate in canon law, which he would earn from the Angelicum in Rome (defended 1987), on *The office and authority of the local prior in the order of Saint Augustine*. In the midst of a displacement requiring him to become familiar with an unfamiliar place and company and culture—Rome, and the Dominican-led hodgepodge of Catholic secular and religious and laity at the "Ang" (as the Pontifical University of St. Thomas Aquinas *in urbe*, the Angelicum, is commonly and most often affectionately known), and his own brethren of the OSA with whom he was living, and the vicissitudes of Roman life in general (about which suffice it for now to say that Rome is the most marvellous place in all the world to live, so long as one need not do anything)—Fr. Robert Francis Prevost OSA was thinking deeply, consecutively, and publicly about the role of the very authority that had sent him to that place, in his life and in the lives of all his Augustinian brethren.

It was quite an ordinary experience, that is, for an Augustinian friar to be sent for advanced study to Rome. The single detail of an irreducible life takes on its air of the uncanny often only in hindsight, when it appears as if the whole of it had not been so much scripted or orchestrated as directed by a power at once so far beyond the world as to defy imagination—let alone comprehension—and so near, intimate, familiar as hardly to be noteworthy, and that shocks us, or can shock us if we let it.[7] Saint Augustine famously described the strangeness of human nature to itself—the real sense of being a stranger to ourselves, which we all have felt at some point very keenly and carry with us every day—as the sense not so much of being lost as of being neither here nor there, a sense often perceptible or discernible only in hindsight: "[F]ar from your immovable stability," Saint Augustine wrote at the very end of the second book of his *Confessions*, "I became to myself a region of destitution.[8]"

Even now, in this moment—the moment of your reading and the moment of this author's writing—the irreducible, inexhaustible complexity of a single human life is discernible, sensible, evident. Charting a course through it is impossible. Even when we find a through-line—if we find one—the finding it puts us perpetually at risk of missing most of what is before us and behind us. "Begin at the beginning," is not bad advice, only where the story really begins is not less difficult to say than it would be to tell the end before we get there. This is true for Pope Leo XIV, as it is for any of us.

(Extra)ordinary beginnings

Robert Francis Prevost entered the world on 14 September 1955 in Chicago, Illinois, the youngest of three boys born to Louis Marius Prevost and Mildred Agnes Prevost (née Martinez). Robert's parents were Chicago natives and lifelong Chicagoans. Both parents were professionally involved in education and devoted to the upbuilding of civic life. Their family's history, not only in their generation, is inextricably interwoven with the history of their native city and their native land.

In collaboration with American Ancestors and the Cuban Genealogy Club of Miami, Prof. Henry Louis Gates, Jr., of Harvard University, traced Pope Leo XIV's ancestry for *The New York Times Sunday Magazine*, which published the findings on 11 June 2025. Gates presented Leo with a copy of his report.

Pope Leo received Gates and his wife, historian Dr. Marial Iglesias Utset, in a special private audience on 5 July 2025. Gates later called the audience "one of the most meaningful and deeply moving moments of our lives." It was a "profound honour," Gates said, to be thus received by the Holy Father and "to present him with a copy of his family tree." Gates offered his comments in his own announcement of the meeting on social media.

"[Dr. Utset] and I had worked with an outstanding team of researchers," Gates also wrote, "and were deeply grateful for the chance to walk His Holiness through the branches of his family tree, sharing stories of his ancestors back to his 12th great-grandparents who were born some 500 years ago." Readers interested in a deeper dive into Pope Leo's genealogy could do far worse than to start with that *Times* write-up. "[T]he pope's roots," Gates reports, "make for one of the most diverse family trees we have ever created." Leo, it turns out, is not only the first pope from the United States, he is the first pope of African-American descent and the first pope with any established claim to African descent since Gelasius I—like Saint Augustine, from Roman North Africa—who reigned from 492–496.

Louis Marius Prevost (28 July 1920–8 November 1997) was a veteran of World War II who volunteered for the US Navy's "V-7" reserve officer training programme in 1942, toward the end of his junior year at Central YMCA College.[9] US war records show Louis was a naval officer who served on a Landing Ship, Tank (LST) during D-Day operations and later a larger troop-carrier in the Mediterranean theatre. After the war, Louis returned to civilian life and continued his education. He earned a Master of Arts degree in education and had a career as an administrator in the Chicago municipal school system.

Mildred Prevost (30 December 1911–18 June 1990) was a trail-blazer in her own right, the mixed-race daughter of Spanish and Afro-French Creole descent—the Spanish by way of Cuba and the French by way of both Quebec and New Orleans—who earned a Master of Science in education in an historical moment at which few women in the United States so much as sought advanced degrees, and fewer women of colour even had the opportunity to do so. Mrs. Prevost worked as a school librarian for much of her life, especially in the Catholic schools of her native Chicago. She was also an amateur singer of some accomplishment who recorded a version of "Ave Maria"—her party piece, to hear her son, Louis Jr., tell it (as he did to the NYT's Julie Bosman for an article published 11 May 2025)—and a stage performer who reportedly shared her talents especially for school fund-raisers. "Millie"—as she was known to family and close friends—married Louis late, by the standards of the day, and had her three children—all boys—in the space of just over four years between 1951 and 1955, when she was in her late 30s and early 40s.

Louis and Millie and their boys—Louis Jr. (b. 1951), John (b. 1954), and Robert—made their home in Dolton, a middle-class suburb just beyond Chicago's South Side city limits. Their home life was serene and supportive, almost idyllic, by every account. Louis Jr. joined the US Navy, drafted into service in 1969, at the height of US involvement in Vietnam and while he was in college (university), after which he studied computer science. John became an educator like both of his parents. "We learned how to cook, we learned how to clean, we learned how to iron clothes," Louis Jr. told the NYT on 11 May 2025. "She taught us all the skills needed to be on your own and support yourself," Louis also said.

Passion for education and dedication to the work of forming young minds and hearts were also something the Prevost boys learned from their parents. "Our whole family was geared toward education," Louis told the NYT in that same interview, in which he also noted how their mother "may have wanted to be a teacher one day," and explained how "that never went to fruition because she got married and had kids." On the other hand, one may, without contesting the accuracy of the eldest Prevost's attestation, note how Millie was most certainly a teacher to her boys. In a conversation with the *Good Morning*

America programme of the US network, ABC, on 9 May 2025, John Prevost recounted how Rob, the youngest of the three Prevost boys, gave sign of his vocation from a very early age. "[Rob] would take our mom's ironing board," John said, "[he would] cover it with a tablecloth, and we would go to Mass." Catholic children have been playing at Mass for centuries, probably since Apostolic times.

There were, however, some mid-twentieth-century particulars to the Prevost boys' domestic version of the game. "If you remember an old-fashioned candy called Necco," John said, "those were the communion wafers." That domestic variation was fairly typical of the epoch's Catholic culture. This author remembers using Necco wafers for play-Mass, as a boy in Connecticut in the late 1970s and early 1980s (Necco being an acronym for the New England Confectionery Company, founded in 1901). Even so, there was an adamantine conviction in the youngest Prevost, as John recalled. "[Rob] knew right away," that he would be a priest. "I don't think he ever questioned it," John told GMA. "I don't think he ever thought of anything else."

Catholic boys in the 1960s still considered the priesthood almost as a matter of course, but for Robert Prevost, the childhood games were not mere fancy. They were practice. "Some of us had considered [the priesthood]," John Doughney—a schoolmate at St. Mary of the Assumption parish school in Dolton, from which they both graduated in 1969—told the *Chicago Sun-Times.* Doughney offered his remarks to the *Sun-Times* for a piece about then-Cardinal Prevost—"From the south suburbs to helping choose the next pope"—published 3 May 2025, ahead of the conclave that elected him. "It was kind of a fantasy for most young men," Doughney told the *Sun-Times.* "For him," I think it was a true calling," Doughney said, "even as a young teenager, he knew what he wanted to do and where he wanted to go."

Robert Francis Prevost remained an Augustinian and completed his formation for the priesthood. He was ordained a priest on 19 June 1982, at the Chapel of St. Monica of the

Augustinians in Rome, by Archbishop Jean Jadot, a Belgian prelate and diplomat who had served in the United States as Apostolic Delegate between 1973 and 1980. Also in 1982, Prevost completed advanced studies in theology at the Catholic Theological Union in his native Chicago, begun after his graduation from Villanova in 1977, and took his M.Div. From there, Prevost went to Rome for his studies in canon law, earning the licentiate in 1984 and the doctorate in 1987.

Cerca y personal: Augustinian, missionary, prior

Robert Francis Prevost OSA, however, recounted how very keenly he experienced the tension of existence, the drama of vocational discernment, in his own person. In a July 2023 interview with Italy's leading TG1 news programme of the RAI network (roughly Italy's version of the BBC), Prevost recounted how he had brought his disquiet over his vocation to his father. "I remember sometimes speaking with my father," Prevost said, "who wasn't exactly a spiritual director," but was an educator. "That was his life," Prevost also said during the interview. In those conversations, Prevost said, they would speak "of very concrete things, like the doubts that can come to a young person: 'Maybe it's better to leave this life, to get married, to have children—to have a normal life, let's say—like the one I saw in my own family," he recalled.

"With his experience, he would speak of things like—let's say—intimacy between him and my mother, and how important it was," Prevost said, "but also about how very important is closeness to Christ in a vocation to the priesthood—to know Jesus, to know the love of God in life—how important it is for all Christians." Prevost said he had heard such and similar "a hundred times" from priests and those responsible for his priestly and religious formation, "but, when my father said it, in a very human but deeply meaningful way, I said [to myself]: Here is something to which I need to listen."

The life of Pope Leo XIV has been one that has seen its share of turbulence, on three continents—North America, South America, and Europe—at different times and in different ways. There was the disruption of Catholic life in the United States during the heady days of the Vatican Council II, which unfolded within a sociocultural context of profound upheaval in US society. There was the poverty and protracted political violence of Peru into which his Order of Saint Augustine missioned him when he was still a young priest. There was the global disquiet of sociopolitical, cultural, and institutional unsettlement in the first quarter of the twenty-first century, at the outset of which he came into the worldwide leadership of the Augustinians.

The New York Times told a terrific story—"terrific" in both the colloquial and the etymological senses of the word—about then-Fr. Prevost standing his ground during the dark and trying days of the *Fujimorato* period in Peru, protecting his people and defusing a potentially very dangerous situation. The 17 May 2025 piece in the NYT recounted how Prevost, leading a group of seminarians on a minibus trip in the mid-1990s (around the time Peru's president, Alberto Fujimori, was going from strongman to dictator), met with a band of soldiers searching for young men to enlist. Emergency measures, ostensibly enacted to deal with an ongoing leftist insurgency, had given the army extraordinary powers to press young men into military service. There was an exemption written into the law, however, for clerics.

"No," one witness recalled Fr. Prevost telling the soldiers, "these young men are going to be priests, they cannot go to the barracks." That story came from Fr. Ramiro Castillo OSA, who witnessed the incident. "When he had to speak, he spoke," the NYT quoted Castillo as saying. Castillo has served most recently as the Regional Vicar of the Augustinians' Vicariate of San Juan de Sahagún in northwestern Peru, but at the time of the incident, Castillo was a seminarian in formation. The terse account in the NYT testifies to two things: the lasting impression made on Castillo by both the incident and Prevost;

the willingness of Prevost not only to speak truth to power but to tap and draw from a secret reserve of moral and physical courage.

Before he received his first missionary assignment to Peru, before he was Fr. Prevost or even officially an Augustinian, Prevost had faced and outfaced another form of cultural and social disruption and disintegration. Prevost had performed admirably during his four years of secondary school (1969–73) at St. Augustine Seminary High School in Laketown Township, MI, a two-hour drive from Chicago along and up the south-eastern shore of Lake Michigan. While at St. Augustine, Prevost was a powerful presence who earned both accolades and respect. "[Prevost] was the valedictorian," schoolmate Bob Schick told CBS Boston-affiliate WBZ News for a 9 May 2025 piece. "He was the student body president. He was in charge of speech and debate," Schick told WBZ.

Schick, who was a freshman at St. Augustine in 1977 when Prevost was a senior, described the upperclassman as a fellow with a capacious aptitude for friendship. "[Y]ou had a lot of freshman kids there who were really scared to be away from home," Schick said, "and Bob [Prevost] was one of the guys, one of the seniors, who took people under his wing." While at St. Augustine, Prevost also began to develop his talents for the unglamorous work of real leadership. He reportedly audited the yearbook, of which he was editor-in-chief his senior year. That yearbook would go on to win an award, which got a mention in the 24 February 1974 edition of the local *Holland Sentinel* newspaper in Michigan.

Prevost's class, however, would shrink from several dozen to only 13 members by the time he graduated. "Some got girlfriends, others got homesick, and others lost their calling," the NYT reported, in that same 17 May 2025 piece that contained the account of the harrowing encounter with Fujimori's soldiers. The shrinking of the class was of a piece with the shrinking Catholic footprint in the United States. It was a harbinger of things to come.

For his undergraduate studies, Prevost was to attend the Augustinians' Tolentine College in Olympia Fields—perhaps a half-hour by car to the south and slightly west of Dolton, his hometown. Tolentine closed its doors the very year he was to have started there. So, he went to Villanova in Pennsylvania instead, where he majored in mathematics and forged new friendships. While at Villanova, Prevost helped found the university's—and the nation's—first collegiate pro-life club, Villanovans for Life, in 1974, the year following the landmark *Roe v. Wade* decision of the US Supreme Court, which made abortion legal in all 50 states of the federal republic.

Prevost's lifelong friend, Robert Dodaro, led the effort to found Villanovans for Life, along with Margaret Mary Filoromo (née Dowdall). Dodaro is a renowned Augustinian priest and scholar. Filoromo lived long enough to see *Roe v. Wade* overturned (on 24 June 2022, with the *Dobbs v. Jackson Women's Health Organization* decision, which did not outlaw abortion but only returned the regulation of abortion to the states, most of which had already created broad legal protections for abortion and several of which had already enshrined a right to abortion in fundamental law), but she exchanged time for eternity on 25 June 2024, after 45 years of marriage and a lifetime of service to the cause of life, for which Villanovans for Life honoured her as part of their 50th anniversary celebrations.

Margaret Mary Filoromo's daughter, Maura Filoromo, told OSV News her mother kept abreast of Robert Prevost's doings. "I have heard about him all my life," Filoromo said in an interview published on 30 May 2025. "She talked about where he was in Peru, when he became head of the Augustinians (prior general), and so on," Filoromo said of her mother. "She was really proud of all he accomplished," she also said. "When he became cardinal less than two years ago," Filoromo recounted, "she said to me, 'My friend could become pope. Wouldn't that be wild?'" Prevost, to hear other friends tell it, did not think his election was on the cards. "I think you'd make a great pope," Fr. Anthony Banks OSA told the NYT he wrote to then-Cardinal

Prevost when news of Pope Francis' passing reached him, "but I hope for your sake you're not elected." Banks told the NYT that Prevost responded: "I'm an American, I can't be elected."

Those friendships and others sustained Prevost through the tumult of the second half of the twentieth century and into the furore of the twenty-first. That service—the quiet kind behind the scenes and away from the limelight, left not undone but well begun and for others to carry forward—came from a spirit of care that recognizes how civilizations come and go, while human souls are made for eternity. It also taught him at once never to shrink from duty in the moment and to take the long view of things. There is something profoundly Catholic (and catholic) about that.

Prior general, bishop, cardinal

Fr. Robert Francis Prevost was elected prior general of the Order of Saint Augustine for the first time on 14 September 2001—his 46th birthday—in Rome, while people in the city and around the globe watched with horror the scenes unfolding in New York, Washington DC, and Pennsylvania, knowing that the world had changed but not even dimly understanding how or how much. This author was a young graduate student in Rome at the time and remembers the bottomless anguish of those awful days. The sheer psychological pressure of being saddled with any global leadership role under such circumstances, even one without the care of souls, is almost too terrible to imagine. Prevost would serve two terms as prior general, during which he travelled extensively, visiting Augustinian works and houses throughout the world. As the head of a global religious order dedicated to missionary work, Prevost had to manage human and material resources on a scale comparable to that of multi-national commercial concerns.

As prior general, Fr. Prevost had to know—and to trust—people of every temper and disposition, from vastly different

backgrounds, facing myriad daily challenges and trying circumstances various in kind and degree. He had to be able to identify
potential leaders and give them the chances they would need
in order to grow, knowing that sometimes they would fail. He
needed to know which problems required his address and he
needed to know how to deal with those problems. He needed
to know which problems he could leave to others, and he
needed to know to whom he should leave them. He needed
to know how to put the best available people in place, how to
get them the resources they needed, and how then to get out
of their way.

Just as important, Fr. Prevost needed to understand how
things worked. He learned the ways of the nations and peoples
he visited, even adopting local costume and sampling local
cuisine, some of it very exotic. While travelling the globe
visiting Augustinian works and houses, he cultivated contacts
in the Church, in government, and in civil society. He would
likely have asked probing questions about finances, not only
in order to understand internal accounting and decision-
making, but also to understand how the relationships between
Church, public, private, and civil society institutions contributed
materially to keep the Augustinian lights on.

After two terms in the leadership of his Order of Saint
Augustine, Fr. Prevost was ready to go home—to Chicago, that
is—and to rest. According to one widely publicized account,
Pope Francis gave him to believe, for a little while, that he would
be able to do just that. Francis had accepted Prevost's invitation
to come celebrate the opening Mass of the Augustinians'
general chapter on 28 August 2013—Saint Augustine of Hippo's
feast day and a solemnity for Augustinians—at which Prevost's
successor would be elected. Prevost recalled Francis saying to
him: "Now, rest." Prevost recalled saying, "Thank you, Holy
Father, I hope to rest," in reply.

Still a priest of the Order of Saint Augustine, Fr. Prevost
returned to Chicago for what would turn out to be a brief
spell, during which he served in the relatively un-taxing roles of

formation director and vicar for the Augustinians' Midwestern US province. On 3 November 2014, however, Francis named Prevost bishop and apostolic administrator of the Diocese of Chiclayo in northern Peru. Fr. Prevost received episcopal orders from the Apostolic Nuncio to Peru, Archbishop James Green, on 12 December 2014, in the cathedral basilica of Our Lady in Chiclayo. There is an interesting reason Bishop Prevost did not immediately become Bishop of Chiclayo. Article 7 of the 1980 treaty between the Holy See and Peru governing Church-state relations requires that all bishops be Peruvian citizens.[10] So, Prevost sought naturalisation and became a Peruvian citizen in August 2015. On 26 September 2015, Prevost officially became Bishop of Chiclayo.

As Bishop Prevost would himself recount in 2023—in leave-taking remarks posted to social media by the Peruvian bishops (who had awarded him their highest honour, the Gold Medal of St. Turibius of Mogrovejo, named after the sainted Dominican friar who was Archbishop of Lima from 1579 until his death in 1606) and widely reported in the wake of the May 2025 conclave that elected him Pope Leo XIV—he expected the 2013 election of Pope Francis should have foreclosed any chance of his becoming a bishop. Austen Ivereigh, Pope Francis' most authoritative biographer, recounted in *Commonweal* an episode[11] in which then-Fr. Prevost and then-Cardinal Bergoglio had a contretemps over personnel—basically, Bergoglio wanted one of Prevost's friars for some work or other, and Prevost told him he could not have his man—but Prevost played a close hand, then and now. "I won't tell you the reason," Prevost said in 2023, "but let's say that not all the meetings [I had] with Cardinal Bergoglio always ended with the two of us in agreement." So, when Bergoglio became Pope Francis in 2013, Prevost remarked: "Well, that's very good, and thank God I'll never be a bishop."

Bishop Prevost would remain in Chiclayo roughly eight years, during which time he cultivated many friendships and working relationships. An Associated Press story published on 9 May 2025 collected anecdotes from people who knew him in Chiclayo—a northwestern city of about 800,000, and a significant commercial hub—telling of a fellow who sang Christmas songs with his people, played tennis, dined in local establishments, and drove—or rode and sometimes walked flooded streets—to reach those in need. Fr. Jorge Millán, who lived with Leo and other brothers in Chiclayo and is now the cathedral rector, spoke to the AP of Leo's "mathematical mindset," saying, "he was orderly and punctual." Millán said Leo did his own dishes and enjoyed working on cars. Millán also told the AP of how the new pope would look for answers on YouTube when some mechanical problem or other had him flummoxed.[12]

"We saw a bishop who put on a helmet, boots and went out to meet people, very close, very, very humble with everyone," Janinna Sesa, a worker for the Church's charitable outreach, Caritas, told NPR's *Morning Edition* on 9 May 2025, "from those who held important positions to the most humble of people." Sesa also recounted to NPR how Prevost proved resourceful and effective as a leader in a time of great crisis.[13] The Chiclayo region was struggling during the Covid-19 pandemic, she said, especially under a shortage of much-needed oxygen. "Thanks to [Prevost's] efforts," Sesa said, "we managed to buy not just one plant, but two oxygen plants," which produced oxygen that was "made available free of charge to anyone who needed it, especially the most vulnerable, and saved many lives."

Pope Francis called him to Rome to serve as Prefect of the Dicastery for Bishops, naming him to the leadership of the powerful curial department at the end of January 2023. Fr. Alejandro Moral Antón OSA, who succeeded then-Fr. Prevost as prior general in 2013 and was re-elected prior general of the Augustinians in 2019, told *The New York Times* Francis had asked him whether he thought Prevost would do well in the job, which is responsible—among other things—for vetting candidates for appointment to dioceses and archdioceses throughout the world and for some disciplinary matters. Moral Antón thought he would do well, and Francis agreed.

Then-Archbishop (soon thereafter to be Cardinal) Prevost moved to Rome and got to work. He impressed his staff with his ability to listen with careful attention and to keep meetings properly focused. Sometimes despite the best efforts of other participants, Prevost would correct course and move matters in the right direction. Insiders noted how Prevost could accomplish these course-corrections often without the meandering and loquacious parties ever becoming the wiser. Shortly after Prevost arrived in Rome and the Vatican to take up work in his new office, however, a story of serious oversight failure broke.

In the year 2000, when then-Fr. Prevost was provincial head of the Augustinians in Chicago, he allowed Fr. James Ray, an accused abuser-priest of the Archdiocese of Chicago, to reside in an Augustinian house—the St. John Stone Friary—situated near an elementary school.[14] Ray, who has never been convicted and is not on any list of sex offenders maintained by Illinois civil government, had allegations against him and had been on restricted ministry for nearly a decade. Reportedly, the Archdiocese of Chicago made note of the restrictions on Ray when requesting hospitality for him in the Augustinians' house. Prevost apparently neither alerted the school, nor caused the school to be alerted. Subsequent reporting by the *Chicago Sun-Times* (which broke the story) quoted Chicago archdiocesan records as incorrectly asserting "there was no school in the immediate area," but the Augustinians ought to have known better and in any case ought to have said something.[15]

The episode with Ray was a serious failure—there is no mistaking it—one that put people in danger. It is also the case, that the episode occurred some two years before the crisis of abuse and cover-up erupted in Boston, with the *Boston Globe*'s "Spotlight" investigative reportage. The Boston scandal quickly engulfed the whole United States and then spread around the world. The crisis of abuse and cover-up—a crisis of clerical and hierarchical leadership culture—is one of very long standing, which persists in the present.

Fr. Hans Zollner SJ, widely considered the Church's leading expert on safeguarding, has said this generation will not live to see the end of it. "This will not be over in our lifetime," Zollner told an audience at Fordham University[16] in March of 2019, "at least in countries where they have not yet started to talk about it." The crisis certainly was with the Church in the year 2000, as then-Fr. Prevost's failure in leadership when he was provincial superior amply though micro-cosmically attests. The scandal of the crisis—the awareness the scandal compelled—was dim on the horizon at best.

Going into the conclave that elected Robert Francis Prevost OSA as Pope Leo XIV, observers across the spectrum of opinion in the Church knew that every prospective candidate's leadership record on abuse and cover-up would be a subject of scrutiny. Many observers wondered whether there would be anyone found in the College with an unblemished record. The answer, most agreed, was a qualified "No." The election of Prevost—a man with an imperfect record, who had already faced significant public scrutiny—may have been in fact a sign of awakening—much-belated so the more welcome—among the cardinals. Their choice of a man, whose skeletons were already out of the closet, was arguably indicative of their awareness not only that their choice would face scrutiny, whoever he was, but that he would have no excuse when the time came for leadership on the crucial issue.[17]

The hand of providence

The Italians have an expression: *L'uomo propone e Dio dispone.* Translated, that says: "Man proposes, and God disposes." The expression contains at once the ideas that "God paints straight with crooked lines," that God determines the outcome within and often despite "the best laid plans of mice and men," and that "God's ways are not man's ways." People who go in for that sort of thing, as this author does, may discover in the crystalline of hindsight a providential power at work throughout the life of Robert Francis Prevost, whose capacity for friendship, for leadership, for plain old hard work, brought him through times that broke men and societies.

In any case, the name of Robert Francis Cardinal Prevost was one apparently under consideration in the official pre-conclave meetings (called general congregations) and the informal gatherings around Roman tables in the run-up to the conclave. From there, it seeped into the Italian rumour mill. Prevost's career, his language skills, missionary background, legal training and experience, all conspired to recommend him. The strong impression Prevost had made during his short tenure as head of a powerful Roman curial department also helped. That Prevost had risen under Pope Francis even though he was known to have clashed with him also made him an attractive candidate.

All the cardinal electors were exhausted after the Francis pontificate—the Church was exhausted after it—but a good number of them thought Francis' programme was one worth pursuing. More of them genuinely appreciated Francis' broad pastoral instincts, even if they found his programme in need of significant adjustment and even seriously problematic, while others thought a change of direction urgently needful. Prevost appeared to the cardinals almost the polar opposite of Francis in terms of character and temperament, which appealed to everyone. Francis saw something in Prevost, even though Prevost sometimes did not see things Francis' way, which made Prevost acceptable to a broad swathe of electors. There is a great deal more to say about the conclave—and there will be more in the chapter to follow—but for now, it is time to consider the great pitch and moment of Pope Leo XIV's first appearance on the *loggia*.

Chapter 3

"Peace be with all of you"

"Peace be with all of you." Those were Pope Leo XIV's first words from the central loggia above St. Peter's Basilica, spoken *in primis*—but by no means solely—to the mix of Romans, pilgrims, and lucky tourists who happened to be in town for the event, all gathered in St. Peter's Square. To hear the Gospel writers Luke and John tell it, they were also the words with which the risen Christ greeted the disciples as they hid together, fearful and unsure of what would come for them after the crucifixion. "Dear brothers and sisters," the new pope said, "these are the first words spoken by the risen Christ, the Good Shepherd who laid down his life for God's flock." Leo, as we were all learning to call him, was also speaking to the worldwide body of the Catholic faithful, to Christians everywhere, and to everyone else on the globe. "I would like this greeting of peace to resound in your hearts, in your families, among all people, wherever they may be," Leo said, "in every nation and throughout the world."

His message was at once *ad intra* and *ad extra*: an unfamiliar expression, perhaps, but one that says nothing arcane. The Latin translates literally as "to the inside" and "to the outside" and conveys the idea that the speaker's message is intended for Catholics and non-Catholics—Christians and non-Christians, believers and unbelievers—of every stripe. The Church speaks to her members (*ad intra*) and to the whole world (*ad extra*) whenever she says anything at all. Pope Leo XIV, the head of the Church on Earth, was using what was effectively (and almost literally) the world's biggest bully pulpit to focus the world's attention on Christ, the Prince of Peace. That was not all he was doing.

Those words set the tone of his pontificate, to be sure. The specific words Pope Leo XIV chose to make his own, were also both immediately accessible to everyone (*ad extra*) and endlessly engaging for people with varying degrees of specialized knowledge, experience with the Church and the papacy, even basic human interest (*ad intra*). To Catholics, churchmen and faithful alike, they were a balm after what had been an exhausting and frequently contentious pontificate. To other Christians, they were a word of consolation in a moment of uncertainty: There are Orthodox, Protestant, Anglican, and even "emerging" Christians deeply wounded by the sad divisions in the worldwide body of the faithful and invested in the work of healing, who were wondering what sort the new pope would be. To people in areas torn by strife, ravaged by poverty, and suffering under persecution, they were a consolation. To the curious, they sounded like something the pope should say.

Pope Leo XIV's first words invited exploration but did not insist on it. Like the words of Jesus, whose words they were before Leo made them his own, they did their surface work and much more. Those six words, however, hid nothing. They contained nothing esoteric, nothing unavailable to anyone willing to listen with as much care as one could muster, but spoke simultaneously and with great clarity on several different levels. They met people where they were, in other words. They disclosed as much or as little as anyone hearing them was or would be prepared or disposed to hear. They were at once perfectly straightforward and inexhaustibly eloquent.

Radically moderate

It is not unhelpful to compare them with his predecessors' choices. Pope Francis offered, "Brothers and sisters, good evening," and then joked—as had Pope St. John Paul II on the night of his own election—about how far the cardinals had gone to find him, before focusing his remarks on the journey of bishop-and-people together, a theme that would become a leitmotiv of his pontificate. "Dear brothers and sisters," Pope Benedict XVI began, before describing himself as "a simple and humble labourer in the vineyard of the Lord" and noting the comfort he took in "the fact that the Lord knows how to work and to act even with inadequate instruments." John Paul II made his exordium with, "Praised be Jesus Christ!" before greeting his "dearest brothers and sisters" in the square and around the world, and remarking the shock and sadness at John Paul I's sudden and unexpected passing, from which he and Catholics worldwide were still reeling.

On one reading, Pope Leo XIV placed himself precisely in the middle of a spectrum running from Pope Benedict XVI's introspective rumination and John Paul II's formulaic Christocentrism, with Pope Francis' greeting rather homespun and an outlier. There is almost certainly something to that reading, but not everything.[18] The New Testament was written in Greek, but Hebrew and Aramaic—the common spoken language in and around the region of Judea—were languages in which "Peace be with you!" was a common greeting. Arabic, too, has a similar convention. The expression is frequently shortened to *Shalom!* (Hebrew) and *Salaam!* (Arabic) when people use them informally. These days, one is likely to hear friends greeting one another with them on the street of almost any city in the world. Francis's use of the Italian, *Buona sera!*— literally, "Good evening!"—was not as much of an outlier as it may have appeared at first blush, therefore, nor were Jesus' own words so solemn as they may strike us today.

Leo's decision to take the risen Christ's words of greeting to the disciples and make them his own first words to the Church, to Christians, and to the world, was therefore a choice for what one might call *radical moderation*. It was a bold choice also in keeping with the deep current of tradition. It was a choice that threaded a needle. As we shall see, it was part and parcel of careful communication that was a master stroke of rhetoric.

The power—and limits—of gestures and signs

Pope Leo XIV made other choices on that day and the days that followed, which everyone watching saw. Not everyone watching noticed the choices as such—at least, not everyone noticed himself noticing them—but they were there and at work. When Leo appeared on the *loggia* above St. Peter's Basilica, for example, he was dressed in the red *mozzetta* and burgundy *stola* with intricate gold embroidery. The *mozzetta*, a deep red shoulder cape (of which there are seasonal variations), has for centuries been one of the principal counter-distinguishing marks of papal office.

Leo looked like the pope, in short. His first appearance was in stark contrast to that of Pope Francis, who had appeared without the *mozzetta* or *stola* over the white cassock, which Francis did wear. Pope Francis chose not to wear the *mozzetta* at all during his reign, and only donned the *stola* when he would give the pontifical blessing *urbi et orbi* ("to the city and to the world"). The white cassock has been the habitual attire of the Roman pontiff since at least the time of Pope St. Pius V—a Dominican who continued to wear his white habit even after his election—with remote origins stretching several centuries earlier, to the time of Pope Gregory X (1271–76).

The red *mozzetta* and the *stola*, however, recall in specific ways peculiar to the Roman pontiff—whoever he is—the nature and scope of the papal office. Leo did not wear them only on the balcony, but has continued to use them when the occasion calls. When Francis eschewed the garments, observers discerned in his decision to forego them not only a sign of simplicity and humility, but of a strong character who would not be bound by convention in his conduct of the Petrine power. Observers took

Pope Leo XIV's choices to indicate a return to convention, not only in the public-facing *persona* of the pope, but also in the modes and orders under which Leo would conduct the office to which he had come in his turn.

Conversations with people within and around the conclave that elected Leo suggest that a return to convention, to a sense of regularity, even predictability, was something high on the list of the cardinal electors' concerns. People across the spectrum of opinion in the Church shared that concern. Leo gave other indications, as well, of his intention to operate within the conventions of the office. There was, from the outset, a hope to see that intention also to show itself through orderly conduct of the papal governing office.

At Mass on 9 May 2025 in the Sistine Chapel, for example, Pope Leo XIV carried the papal *ferula*—the special pastoral staff peculiar to the Roman pontiff—that had been designed for Pope Benedict XVI and is particularly associated with Benedict and his reign. Leo wore liturgical vestments that day, which had been designed for Pope Francis.[19] The choices were certainly conciliatory, therefore an implicit recognition of tension and even division within the Church, or perhaps of fault lines. They were also indicative—perhaps—of Leo's intention to harmonize the voices, ideas, personalities, even agenda, which had become discordant in the Church of late.

Pope Leo XIV's words and gestures in the first days of his pontificate were radical in the sense of the Latin *radix*, for root. They sprang from Christ and focused attention on Christ's resurrection, then on the office of Peter in the Church, which Christ had established. They evinced real sensibility of the precise historical moment, in which Leo had come to play a protagonist's role. They were moderate both in the sense that they were measured—carefully calibrated—and in that they were profoundly thoughtful, considerate of the men who had elected him—in very short order—their dissonant opinions notwithstanding, and of the faithful over whom he had come to rule. They were conciliatory and consoling, though they were not surprising, which was perhaps the most startling thing about them.

In order to understand why they were not surprising, but were nonetheless startling, it is necessary to understand a thing or two about the College of Cardinals, the body that has elected the pope since the twelfth century. The origins of the College reach as far back as the eighth century and even before, ultimately to the establishment of the clerical hierarchy in the diocese of Rome, itself. Even so, the College of Cardinals has not always existed in the Church. In theory, the College could be abolished, though not without significant trouble for pretty much everyone. The composition and responsibilities of the College have varied much through the centuries of its existence, as have the requirements for membership in it.

Strange bedfellows: The College of Cardinals in brief

You will sometimes hear cardinals called "red hats" because of the colour—"cardinal" red, a hue that has actually changed more than a little through the years—associated with their status. Their red hats and red dress are a sign of their special closeness to the Roman pontiff—the pope—whose official colour until the late Middle Ages was not white, but red (something preserved in the papal *mozzetta* and in other trappings of papal office). Becoming a cardinal is not something that happens by means of ordination. Cardinals are rather "created" much as nobles may be created, and cardinals are in fact sometimes called "princes of the Church" in acknowledgment of their status (though it is a mode of address discouraged these days). The red particularly signifies a cardinal's readiness to be faithful *usque ad effusionem sanguinis*—even unto the shedding of [their own] blood—to keep faith, in other words, with the Catholic Faith.

The title, Cardinal, comes from *cardo*—"hinge" in Latin— originally evocative of the pivotal role cardinals play in the Church of Rome. Formally, in fact, cardinals are the "clergy of Rome" who historically have elected the city's bishop, the Roman pontiff. Even today, cardinals are given titular churches in Rome, of which they formally "take possession" when they receive their assignments, even though most of the roughly 250 living cardinals live outside the city. More precisely, titular churches go to cardinal priests, while "deaconries" go to cardinal deacons. Then, there is a third rank—the highest and most exclusive—of "cardinal bishops" who historically have been the nominal heads of the so-called suburbicarian sees around Rome[20]; Pope Francis raised a few cardinals covering senior curial roles to membership in the rank of cardinal bishops during his reign, including one Robert Francis Cardinal Prevost OSA, on 5 February 2025.

The College of Cardinals is the body of senior churchmen, therefore, who are the closest collaborators of the pope. Members of the College who have not reached their 80th birthday by the time the See of Rome becomes vacant, are the cardinals who elect the pope when the time comes. The cardinals who have already reached the age of 80, however, continue to advise the pope while there is one and participate as they are willing and able in the discussions that precede a conclave when the See of Peter is vacant. A cardinal who has turned 80 may also continue to serve as Dean of the College of Cardinals, even though he may not participate in a papal conclave.[21] In the conclave that elected Robert Francis Prevost OSA as Pope Leo XIV, the cardinal secretary of state, Pietro Parolin, presided in place of the dean (the 91-year-old Giovanni Battista Cardinal Re).

Pope Francis greatly expanded voting membership in the College of Cardinals. There were 133 cardinal-electors in the conclave that elected Francis' successor, more than in any other conclave in history, and 13 more than the limit of 120 first established by Pope St. Paul VI.[22] Until the last century, however, the College of Cardinals was a largely European and mostly Italian body. The archbishops of certain major cities would typically receive a red hat, in acknowledgment of the importance of the Church in the city and the country. It was a very big deal, for example, when Archbishop John McCloskey of New York received the red hat from Bl. Pius IX in 1875, making McCloskey the first cardinal from the United States. All throughout the twentieth century, popes expanded not only the numerical but also the demographic constitution of the College, adding members from every habitable continent. Pope Francis used the red hat to recognize Churches—not only or even primarily the pastoral leaders, but the Catholic communities they led—on the "peripheries" as he liked to say, often in impoverished areas of the global south, many of which daily face serious difficulties and even persecution because of their faith.

Basically, the College of Cardinals had been changing not only in its composition but in its purpose, for about a hundred years. From its twelfth-century origins as a body of senior Roman clerics whose special duty it was to elect the pope and advise him on matters of government, to an extension of the papal office throughout Europe (mostly), the College—and the cardinalate—had become a privileged representation of the universal Church to her earthly head. Seen in that light, the expansion of the College and the inclusion of so many from all around the world was a frank—and frankly overdue—acknowledgment of reality. The Church's centre of gravity had shifted, while the papal office itself, once a Roman office with universal jurisdiction, was increasingly a global office centred in Rome. It again bears mention in this regard, that Robert Francis Prevost OSA, represented the Church in the Americas as a cardinal who came in some sense from both the US and Peru (and covered a senior billet in the Roman Curia—Prefect of the Congregation for Bishops—which evaluates candidates for the episcopacy and handles some episcopal disciplinary matters).

On the other hand, Pope Francis convened the whole College of Cardinals only very infrequently. Popes would typically convene the whole College for two purposes: to seek their advice on some important matter or matters, often with bearing on the whole Church; to give them a chance to meet and get to know one another. Those meetings—called consistories, the name also used for gatherings when the pope creates new cardinals—are also opportunities for cardinals from far-flung places to get a feel for how things really work in Rome. Since there had been relatively few "get-to-know-you" consistories during the reign of Francis, and since Francis had created so many cardinals from parts of the world traditionally underrepresented in the College, observers were unsure of the cardinals' ability to reach consensus in short order. There were too many men unfamiliar with each other, the line of thinking ran, too many men whose opinions and character and temperament were untested. The idea was that the constitution of the College in May 2025 made for a wide-open field, and that would mean a messy—perhaps a protracted—election.

Pope Francis had created roughly eight in ten of the cardinal electors participating in the conclave that chose his successor. Francis created them, however, not so much with a view to their affinity or sympathy with his programme, as he did with a view to their representative power, which cut both ways. The cardinals Francis created represented the pope's concern for the people on the peripheries. They also represented those peripheries to the pope at the centre of power in the universal Church. One practical upshot of this iconographical valence Francis had not so much given as developed in the College, it turned out, was that its members gravitated around a figure with whom they had at least passing acquaintance: Robert Francis Cardinal Prevost OSA.

The conclave of May 2025 in context

Papal conclaves are secret affairs, the inevitable politicking of them shrouded in mystery and the subject of mostly ill-informed conjecture. The mechanics of them, however, are determined by law and are well known. Conclaves begin in the afternoon on a day determined by the cardinals in general congregation—usually no fewer than 15 days after the papal office has become vacant—and there may be a round of voting on the first day. The voting proceeds, two rounds in the morning and two in the afternoon, for three days. If there is no election after three days of balloting, there is to be a pause in voting for a maximum of one whole day. Also, and crucially, popes are elected by a two-thirds majority.

Pope Leo XIV was elected on the first ballot of the afternoon on the second day of the conclave—two days, four ballots—making the conclave comparable in length to those which elected both of his most recent predecessors. Pope Francis was elected on the second ballot of the afternoon on the second day of his: two days, five ballots. Pope Benedict XVI was elected, like Leo, also on the first ballot of the afternoon on the second day. The similarities, however, end there.

For one thing, the conclave that elected Pope Benedict XVI was composed of cardinals choosing the successor to a man almost universally beloved of the faithful, whose presence on the world stage had been titanic. More to the point, the faithful present at John Paul II's funeral all but declared him a saint by acclamation. *Santo subito!* was the cry in the square and all the way down the jam-packed *Via della Conciliazione*. The choice of Joseph Cardinal Ratzinger—right-hand man and theological *eminence grise* to John Paul II, the philosopher-priest and likely saint—was not unexpected. More prosaically, there was the fact that John Paul II had changed the rules of papal elections so that a simple majority could elect the pope after 33 ballots, if only a simple majority of cardinal electors agreed to adopt the simple majority election rule at that point. Practically speaking, the backers of any given candidate only needed a simple majority, so long as they were willing to hold out until the 33rd round of voting, so the college would fall in line as soon as a simple majority candidate emerged.

Pope Benedict XVI removed John Paul II's simple majority modification in 2007, restoring the absolute requirement of a two-thirds majority. Churchmen and observers alike approved Benedict's decision, essentially because the election of any man to fill so powerful an office as the papacy ought to have broad support or at least acquiescence. Benedict, however, would eventually do the unthinkable and renounce the papal throne, throwing the whole Church into great turmoil. It was February 2013 when he did, and I was working at Vatican Radio at the time, on the English news desk.[23] When the cardinals convened to elect Benedict's successor in March 2013, everyone was still trying to figure out which way was up. By all reports, Jorge Mario Cardinal Bergoglio SJ had given a good showing in the 2005 conclave that elected Benedict. The cardinals chose Bergoglio to succeed Benedict as Pope Francis, and one may be forgiven the impression they were somehow, on some level, wondering whether they had not chosen the wrong man the last time.

Then, there was the fact that the Francis pontificate had been extremely turbulent and powerfully polarizing. Francis was forcefully challenging to the faithful and to the world, not least in his championship of people and causes he felt were deserving of much better from governments and civil society as well as from Christians generally and Catholics in particular. Francis was willing not only to tolerate but to support the efforts of daring and unconventional pastoral workers in difficult mission fields. Media coverage of Pope Francis—both in the Catholic press and in the secular mainstream—had focused on his "maverick" style of leadership, his mastery of the grand gesture, his avuncular charm, and his inveterate capacity for quotable homespun. In every respect, Francis was great for copy, favourable and unfavourable.

Pope Francis' ecological advocacy, his efforts to advance interreligious dialogue, his constant support for migrants and itinerant peoples, were never going to be universally appreciated in the Church. That was not so much because Christians tend to think those issues unimportant in general. In part, it was because they are prudential matters: people who do agree on the principles undergirding necessary moral commitment to responsible care of the created order, for example, may disagree on how best to go about caring for creation. In part, it was because the issues Francis championed were often the darlings of powerful cultural forces in the developed world, forces often perceived—and then often rightly—as unfriendly to Christian faith and morality. Rightly or wrongly, Francis was happy enough to let himself be something of a figurehead for the cultural elite.

Rightly and wrongly, some Catholics sometimes chafed at his willingness to be so used, and some of them perceived in his willingness an inversion of priorities, as though the relevance of Christianity were in its usefulness to a given sociopolitical agenda. That perception was false, in the main, but Pope Francis did little to dispel it and even sometimes encouraged it. He would decry abortion as tantamount to contract murder, for example, and also describe the likes of Emma Bonino, an anticlerical radical politician and great champion of legal abortion in Italy, as "great" for her service to her country. For Francis, always, people were primary. All other considerations gave way to the cultivation of personal relationships.

The attitude Pope Francis struck, therefore, was inevitably frustrating on occasion. When and where mere matters of public relations and media coverage were concerned, the frustrations were mostly momentary and manageable, even sometimes to advantage. They did reach a saturation point. Catholics who had been willing to give Francis a chance eventually grew tired of waiting for him to declare which side he was on, really. They may have been willing indefinitely to shrug their shoulders at Francis' unlikely behaviour as so much skylarking, but Francis' cheerleaders both official and unofficial frequently responded to expressions of perplexity with accusations of disloyalty and even sinister motivation. It was not an edifying spectacle.

The priority Pope Francis gave to personal relationships was frustrating especially to more politically and socially conservative observers both within and without the professional Catholic

47

press fold, but could have been a minor quirk of a radically new and different personal style of communication. Pope Francis, however, preferred personal to institutional rule. It encompassed his modes of governance, in other words, and that was a problem even—sometimes especially—for churchmen broadly sympathetic to his commitments and agenda. Francis' preference for personal rule led him to ignore, sidestep, sometimes even egregiously to flout the traditional constraints of the papal office, unleashing enormous energy but also dissipating it quickly and dangerously. There was little regularity in the way Francis governed the Church, and that caused problems for everyone.

In any case, unity and a return to convention and to regularity were things for which most cardinal electors were very keen. Unity, that is, understood not as uniformity but "a firm and profound communion in diversity, provided that full fidelity to the Gospel is maintained," as the Dean of the College of Cardinals, Giovanni Battista Re, put it in his homily during the Mass for the election of the Roman pontiff—the *Missa pro eligendo Romano pontifice*—on 7 May 2025, the day the cardinals entered the conclave. The cardinals were looking for regularity understood not only as predictability and order in the conduct of affairs, but as rule of law, which Pope Francis had frequently praised as a necessary pillar of justice and bulwark or order in the Church as in any society, even as he frequently wielded the law as a political tool. Pope Francis, in fact, had enacted sweeping reform legislation touching almost every area of ecclesiastical life, but also frequently excepted, exempted, or otherwise sidestepped or simply chose not to apply his own laws to specific cases.

In the area of financial reform, for example, Francis gave a sweeping mandate to George Cardinal Pell of Australia, then sided with the exponents of the Old Guard in the Vatican almost every time Pell clashed with them, leaving Pell's wings clipped almost as soon as he had begun his work. By the time Pell stepped away from his billet in the Secretariat for the Economy to fight spurious charges of sexual abuse in his native and beloved Australia, he was already odd man out. Pell's decision to return and face the protracted legal ordeal that would eventually see him vindicated in Australia's highest court—though not before he spent 404 days in prison—was nothing if not courageous and principled. Francis offered little in the way of public statements of support for Pell during his ordeal, and he faced rough treatment in the press for his prudent reserve. Francis did let Pell keep his appointment as Prefect of the Secretariat for the Economy, however, until it expired in 2019. That decision was perhaps itself a show of personal support for the embattled cardinal and a testament to Francis' preference of the personal over the institutional, but it stalled his financial reform irretrievably.

Pope Francis' record of leadership in the Church's fight against sexual abuse and cover-up was frankly dismal. Francis issued paper reforms ostensibly designed to strengthen ecclesiastical investigative scope and methods and streamline prosecutions, then used his new law only very sparingly, even selectively, and with a degree of opacity irreconcilable with reason, incompatible with the appearance of justice, and repugnant to plain common sense.[24] Francis promised an "all-out battle" against the scourge of abuse and cover-up in the Church, then allowed Jean-Pierre Cardinal Ricard, a self-confessed child molester, to remain in the clerical state and even to keep his red hat.[25] Francis protected Bishop Gustavo Oscar Zanchetta, an Argentinian prelate Francis himself made a bishop in 2013, who was eventually convicted—by an Argentinian criminal court— of criminal sexual misconduct against his own seminarians, and sentenced to more than four years in prison.[26] In the case of Archbishop Michel Aupetit of Paris, Francis accepted his resignation "not on the altar of truth, but on the altar of hypocrisy"—Francis' own words—before a police investigation completely exonerated Aupetit.[27]

More generally, Pope Francis' piecemeal reforms of the Roman Curia and of the body of law governing religious

congregations—their establishment, government, and disso-
lution—was unwieldy in design and unevenly applied.[28] Francis'
reform of marital nullity law proved difficult and in some places
impossible to implement because of other existing special law.[29]
Completed under Francis and with his input, the wholesale
revision of the Church's penal law—Book VI of the Code of
Canon Law, promulgated in 2021—while it had many elements
experts found praiseworthy, nevertheless contains inexplicable
lacunae and insensible omissions.[30] As a legislator, in short,
Francis' unsystematic approach created serious problems in and
across a broad swathe of areas. His penchant for personal rule
made him an uneven and unpredictable governor.

From the outside looking in, Catholics—churchmen and
laity alike—often vaguely sensed more than they clearly saw the
problems Pope Francis' ersatz governance created. Combined
with his scattershot approach to spoken communication,
especially on matters requiring both doctrinal precision and
pastoral sensitivity, all that created a potent brew. There were
also elements in the public Catholic sphere actively hostile
to Francis. The vociferous defensive and often reactionary
posture of Francis' most zealous defenders, combined with the
impatience and ill temper of his implacable critics, and with
a curated secular media narrative of Francis as the maverick
reformer and poster boy for pet liberal social causes added
to the mix, all together generated a great deal of heat and
comparatively little light during Francis' reign.

Confusion of the teaching power of the papacy with the
governing power of papal office, both on Pope Francis' part
and in the broad general Catholic public, resulted in an acrid
public discourse. It engendered serious misunderstanding, not
only of Francis but of the challenges facing the Church. It
also had a chilling effect throughout the Roman ecclesiastical
establishment. This confusion was encapsulated and epitomized
in what were unarguably the five most widely quoted and
misunderstood—or misconstrued—words of the entire Francis
pontificate, which he uttered during a press conference en

route to Rome from Rio de Janeiro after World Youth Day on 28 July 2013: "Who am I to judge?"

Pope Francis' deployment of that rhetorical question made him a media darling of the secular mainstream and earned him enormous goodwill among progressive Catholics who believed—or said they believed—the words augured a radical change in Church teaching on homosexuality. The words also did little to assuage the fears of many conservative and traditional Catholics who had already begun to look askance at Francis. The reality of those words was that they revealed a great deal about the way Francis made governance decisions. They said little about the man whose vicissitudes occasioned the remark.

That man was Msgr. Battista Ricca, an Italian prelate appointed by Pope Francis to a sensitive position inside the Institute for the Works of Religion (the IOR for short, often styled the "Vatican Bank"). Ricca had a very spotty record from his time in service with the diplomatic corps of the Holy See. Francis, on the basis of only a very cursory perusal of his case file, decided to trust him. In fairly short order, it emerged that the Apostolic Nuncio under whom Ricca had served in Uruguay had noted grave ambiguities in Ricca's personal conduct. Ricca, in fact, had made himself known to the local police as a frequenter of Montevideo's gay cruising district, among other things. Ricca, in short, was not a test case for inclusivity but a potential security risk who perhaps ought not be appointed to sensitive posts. That was a story in which everyone ought to have been interested, but it was a complicated one, and an already polarized public wanted a simple narrative with clear sides.[31]

Basically, everything good that one heard about Pope Francis was true. In his public and pastoral persona, Francis was powerfully charismatic, pastorally daring, relentlessly hard-working, intensely devoted to people. He was also autocratic, splenetic, unsystematic—not to say disorganized—officious, peremptory, mercurial. As I put it, roughly, in my obituary for Francis: He contained multitudes.

Pope Francis was a true son of St. Ignatius Loyola, who desired the men of his Company to be "pope's men" from first to last, and also that they be fearless theological and pastoral soldiers tethered by perfect devotion to the Petrine office as they seek God in all things, bringing Him greater glory and winning souls for heaven, especially in places where the Church has little institutional presence. As a Jesuit in the See of Peter—the head of the Church's hierarchical leadership—Francis was constantly at risk of breaking that fundamental Ignatian spiritual tension, either by collapsing it or by exploding it. Francis grasped the notion that it were a fool's errand to govern the universal Church as though it were a religious province, but he frequently did govern as though he were a Jesuit superior and the Church—bishops and faithful—his personal Jesuit assistancy.[32]

The conclave that elected Pope Leo XIV was not so much a referendum on his predecessor, as it was an acknowledgment of the good and the ill in the Francis pontificate. The cardinals were not looking for someone to continue with the agenda Francis had set out and pursued. They were not looking for someone who would repudiate that agenda. They were looking for someone with a fighting chance at bringing peace to the Church: order to her affairs and justice to her people. They chose Robert Francis Cardinal Prevost OSA.

Vicar of Christ: The man and the office

The pope—whoever he is—stands in the place of Christ. The pope, to say it with Catholics, is Christ's vicar on Earth. How a given pope fills the office and conducts himself in it, is very much a matter subject to the peculiarities—not to say the vagaries and vicissitudes—of the officeholder: of his character, temperament, age, intelligence, experience, and a host of other considerations too numerous to list. The papacy is an office unlike any other on Earth, it is true, but in one regard at least, it is exactly like every other office: a human being must fill it.

The papal office will change a man (as much as any other office will change a man, and more than any other that comes to mind), and any man who holds the papal office for any length of time will not only bring himself to it but leave something of himself in it. John Paul II profoundly reshaped the papacy in the twentieth century, putting the office in form for action in a world characterized by conflict among mass movements along ideological lines and instantaneous mass communication across borders, unprecedented ease of travel, the post-revolutionary expansion of industrial civilization, simultaneous aging and rejuvenation of global population, *inter alia*. Benedict XVI reigned as a teaching pope at a moment that called for a strong and capable governor, and gave up the office when he came to feel he could not do otherwise. Francis, elected with a mandate to reform the Roman Curia—that is, the Catholic Church's central governing and administrative apparatus—undertook a radical reimagination of the Church's modes and orders in the world, a generational project dubbed synodality, at which he worked a dozen years and barely made a start.

How the office will change Pope Leo XIV, and how Pope Leo XIV will change the papal office, are both questions at present unanswerable. It will be for historians to answer them when his reign is over. Robert Francis Prevost, however, was the man the cardinals chose to succeed Pope Francis in St. Peter's see. Who is he?

The short answer: He is a missionary priest of the Order of Saint Augustine and a bishop, a native of Chicago who lived most of his life far from the country of his birth and chose citizenship of the country—Peru—in which he ministered for many years, a fellow who had leadership put upon him (and was glad every time he could put off the mantle). He is also a polyglot who listens far more than he speaks, an inveterate traveller who has chosen the long slow road over speedier means of conveyance when he has been able to do so.[33] He is a fellow who came late to high rank in the organization to which he early decided to give the whole of his life, quite to his own surprise. He is a fellow who has "seen the elephant" as old soldiers say of their comrades who have witnessed and participated in mighty and terrible battles, and kept himself when and where others have not.

Robert Francis Prevost is also a fellow who has made missteps in leadership. No one is perfect. One mark of a good leader is that he not only learns from his mistakes—we may all do that—but that he lives in awareness of his own limitations and surrounds himself with lieutenants able and willing to tell him when he is at risk of going wrong, when he is not seeing what he needs to see. A senior leader—a head man—must also be able to identify and appoint other senior leaders to powerful positions around the world, and Leo's experience both in his Order of Saint Augustine and at the Dicastery for Bishops apparently spoke well for him in those respects. The cardinals who elected him believed him promising in these regards, but only time and events will tell whether Leo is the kind of leader his electors hoped he would prove to be.

Chapter 4

An Augustinian pope

"I am an Augustinian," Pope Leo XIV said in his first greetings from the *loggia* above St. Peter's Basilica, "a son of Saint Augustine." When he uttered that sentence, Leo said more than the mere words suggest. Leo was acknowledging how he is steeped in the spirituality of the Order of Saint Augustine, mendicant society of clerics founded in the thirteenth century. In one of the great ironies of history, the Order of Saint Augustine is the order of religious priests to which the German reformer, Martin Luther, belonged (until he didn't). Leo XIV is the first Augustinian pope, making his election a peculiar sort of "second first" in a row: consecutive popes, both the first to be elected to the See of Peter from their respective religious orders.

Augustinians, as they are colloquially known, live according to a monastic Rule originally developed by Saint Augustine of Hippo, a great bishop of Hippo Regius, an ancient city in what was then Roman North Africa. Saint Augustine became a bishop at the end of the fourth century AD and the beginning of the fifth, in a time of immense upheaval, profound socio-political disruption, cultural and ecclesiastical confusion, and creeping institutional rot. Saint Augustine lived and worked in what would prove to be the waning years of Roman power in the West. In many ways, the times of Saint Augustine were very eerily similar to our own.

In fact, a significant part of the reason for which Church watchers (including this one) thought it impossible that Prevost should have been elected at all, was that the United States is too powerful an actor on the world stage. Cardinals would not pick anyone from the United States, the conventional wisdom ran, because it would risk concentrating and confusing the moral stature of the papal office with US geopolitical power. Such a juxtaposition—in essence a combination—would harm both, but especially the papacy. Francis Cardinal George, Archbishop of Chicago from 1997 – 2014 and a giant of the US episcopate who died in 2015 after a lengthy and by all accounts heroic battle with cancer, was widely quoted as having said the election of a pope from the United States would only happen after the US entered permanent decline. As I noted in a piece for *Crux* shortly after Leo's election, one formidable question for would-be readers of the signs of the times is now whether we have seen the College contradict the wisdom attributed to the late Cardinal George, or whether we have seen it confirmed.[34]

It is sobering to consider that, when Saint Augustine became Bishop of Hippo in (or about) 395, the sack of Rome in 410 by the army of the Visigoth king, Alaric, was fifteen years away. That event would send shock waves through the whole Empire and be the proximate occasion of Augustine's *magnum opus, On the City of God against the Pagans* (commonly known as the *City of God*). Even after the sack of Rome in 410, however, other Roman men of letters continued to project confidence.[35] In 395, the collapse of Roman imperial order in the West was only eighty-one years off, but imperial citizens were going about imperial life convinced of Rome's inevitability. It is more than a little dangerous to practice any reading of the tea leaves, but the Augustinian mind steeped in history cannot really fail to have the thought occur to it.

Power and order in the Augustinian mind

Saint Augustine of Hippo was deeply preoccupied, in any case, with questions of social order. Saint Augustine was at pains to understand the role of the Church in relation to civil or temporal power—in a word, political power as we understand it today—and the role of Christians in society generally. Saint Augustine, in short, had an abiding concern for peace—its nature, conditions of possibility, limits and constraints—in human affairs. That, by the way, is another reason for which one ought not take surprise at Robert Francis Prevost's choice of words with which to greet the faithful and the world as Pope Leo XIV.

Peace—*pax* in Latin—is not for an Augustinian the mere absence of war. Peace is the presence of justice. Peace, for Saint Augustine, is *tranquillitas ordinis*—the "tranquillity of order"—by which Saint Augustine means a right disposition of things, minds, and affairs both public and private. It is, in other words, a right ordering of thought, desire, action, activity, and circumstance.

That is a tall order, as anyone with a serviceable mirror and the gumption to use it will admit. To achieve any part of it is the work of a lifetime. More to the point, progress in ordering any one area, whether of one's own life or of society, will always at once bear and depend upon the condition of every other. Getting one's priorities straight, for example, may help one act differently. The thing is, thinking clearly and with the ruthless honesty necessary to the task of rightly ordering one's priorities is difficult, even on a good day. That kind of thinking about one's own desires and motives is often impossible, even on the best of days.[36]

We have all tied ourselves in knots attempting to justify or rationalise something we knew we ought not do but really wanted to do anyway. Usually, this has meant no more than that we've found ourselves groggy and out of sorts after an evening of too much fun with friends. Occasionally, successful attempts at self-deceit wreck marriages and break up families, ruin good businesses, and destroy friendships. Every so often, a few people operating under such delusions have the wherewithal to bring the whole world to the brink of financial ruin or to plunge the whole human race into war. It is only human nature, after all, and there is a lot of that going around.

"Peace is built in the heart and from the heart," Leo said to diplomats on 16 May 2025, "by eliminating pride and vindictiveness and carefully choosing our words." In an Augustinian register, that is something quite the opposite of our age's default sentimentalism. Saint Augustine knew that there is no end to the work of uprooting pride and vindictiveness in our hearts—none this side of celestial Jerusalem, at any rate—and also that the achievement of what humility and good-will as we may attain in this life, is really the work of God in us. Peace requires reform of the heart—reform of the soul—and reform of the human heart, like reform of the Church, is ceaseless work that we must undertake while we are on the way. This, by the way, is a further indication of the rhetorical brilliance of Leo's very first words from the *loggia*: "Peace be with all of you."

The key to understanding what Leo meant when he said that peace is built in the heart and from the heart, is in understanding what Saint Augustine means when he says "heart"—hence what Augustinians mean when they say it—in essence the seat of our inmost desire, which is God himself, always waiting for us, endlessly knowable, in the fathomless profundity of the human heart, which means we are never done knowing either God or ourselves.[37]

One commonwealth of all Christians: *In illo uno unum*

"There really is but one commonwealth of all Christians," Saint Augustine says in his *On the Work of Monks* (*De opere monachorum*, written c. 400), which was one of the works that informed what became the Rule of Saint Augustine that informs the life of Pope Leo XIV's Order of Saint Augustine. All Christians together constitute one commonwealth—one *res publica* (sometimes given as *respublica*) in Latin, from which we have the English "republic"—a fact of which Augustine happened to be reminding some shiftless monks who were using their lofty spiritual station as an excuse to do no work, basically admonishing them to earn their keep by contributing to the common good, and permitting them to accept the gifts of the faithful offered in gratitude and solidarity. It bears mention in this context, that Leo's episcopal motto channels and riffs on this notion of universal corporate unity. *In illo uno unum*: "We are One in Him, who is The One".

Citizenship in the Church and citizenship in the many political societies that are constituted in the temporal order of human affairs are never perfectly separable. This is the case in the present, in myriad ways, if only we pay attention. One thinks of the regular and official harassment of Christians in China, the gruesome wholesale slaughter of Christians in Nigeria, the semi-official persecution of Christians in India, to name only a few of the too many places in which confessing Christ crucified and risen is always dangerous and too often too dear. One also thinks of the woman arrested and charged in 2022 for praying outside an abortion clinic—silently and on a public footpath, and outside the clinic's hours of operation—in King's Norton, Birmingham, before being released, seeing the charges dropped, and receiving a payout as well as an apology from police.

It is also—and therefore—present every time one goes to church or says grace or crosses oneself in public or wears a crucifix unmolested and indeed unworried. The two citizenships—of the spiritual order and the temporal—are distinct and even very different. Citizenship of heaven is incompatible with citizenship of the world, but membership in the Church and responsible participation in the civil order of society need not be incompatible with each other (though they are always in tension). The Augustinian knows this even when he is not thinking about it.

Pope Leo XIV has given powerful indication of his abiding concern with the challenge of Christian witness and the preservation of institutional and cultural orders in which everyone is free to serve the common good as a fully responsible participant in society—in a word, as a citizen—Christians, included. In a 21 June 2025 address to the Inter Parliamentary Union, he invoked the great English jurist and statesman, Thomas More, as an example in these regards. "Sir Thomas More was a man faithful to his civic responsibilities," Leo said, "a perfect servant of the state precisely because of his faith, which led him to view politics not as a profession but as a mission for the spread of truth and goodness." Quoting the 31 October 2000 Apostolic Letter of Pope St. John Paul II declaring More the patron of lawyers and statesmen, Leo noted how Thomas More "placed his public activity at the service of the person, especially the weak and poor; he handled social disputes with an exquisite sense of justice; he protected the family and defended it with strenuous commitment; and he promoted the integral education of youth."

"The courage he showed by his readiness to sacrifice his life rather than betray the truth," Pope Leo XIV said, "makes him, also for us today, a martyr for freedom and for the primacy of conscience." Sir Thomas More died a martyr under King Henry VIII on 6 July 1535. He was canonised along with St. John Fisher, bishop and martyr, on 19 May 1935. That Leo saw fit to invoke him mere days after the passage of a bill legalising assisted suicide in the UK, was a fact noteworthy and perhaps telling, not of what Leo believes to be coming but of how he views the very present moment of tension between Christian conviction and public order.

Journeying together

Still on the *loggia*, just after his election, Pope Leo XIV made his own the words Saint Augustine spoke to the people of Hippo in Roman North Africa when he became their bishop: "With you I am a Christian, and for you I am a bishop." This was the sense in which, Leo said, "All of us can journey together toward the homeland that God has prepared for us." As was the case with Leo's unsurprising but startling first words, the words that followed contained much more than their prosaic sense conveyed. His mention of journeying together was certainly

a nod to Pope Francis, who frequently spoke of synodality—
a keystone of his pontificate—as "journeying together." To
understand the fullness of their import, however, will be the
work of years informed by action, ultimately though not exclusively Leo's own, in the conduct of the office to which Leo has
only recently been elected.

Pope Leo XIV: Two keys to understanding

Anyone observing this Leonine pontificate with a view to
comprehension must understand two things. The first is that
Leo thinks carefully about how his words will strike hearers
of different stripes. The second is that Leo sees the world
through an Augustinian lens, and Saint Augustine of Hippo
was as clear-eyed and unsparing an observer of human nature
as ever has trod the earth. Interpreting the pontificate of a
man steeped in such a spiritual tradition and formed in such a
mould will be a daunting task, but not one at which Catholics
are unpractised even in roughly contemporary times. Pope
Benedict XVI, who reigned from April 2005 until the end of
February 2013, was an Augustinian in his intellectual formation
and general outlook.

Benedict XVI, however, was a secular (i.e., diocesan) priest
and a professional theologian with little experience in pastoral
office before he became Archbishop of Munich and Freising
in 1977. Benedict served in that role only four and a half years,
before Pope St. John Paul II called him to service in the Vatican
as Prefect of the Congregation for the Doctrine of the Faith.
Pope Leo XIV, by contrast, has been a religious priest and
missionary somehow engaged in pastoral ministry throughout
nearly the whole of his priestly life. That is a difference that
makes a difference.

The difference it makes is not unlike that which distinguishes
the academic law professor from the lawyer who earns his living
at first instance trial before a jury. The difference between the

professor and the trial lawyer is not necessarily one of intelligence, learning, curiosity, patience, or wit. The difference is in the kind of real-life experience they have, not only as a matter of personal history but of daily habit. The law professor is steeped in theoretical concerns that arise from the everyday but come to the academic in rarefied form; the professor's advice may be indispensable to the law student and precious to the lawyer preparing an appeal to be argued before a panel of judges. The lawyer who tries cases before juries, however, must be able to understand—from the inside, out—and persuade not a panel of judges but a hodgepodge of workaday strangers from different walks of life. If it helps, think of it as the difference between the fictional twentieth-century legal eagles Charles Kingsfield and Horace Rumpole.

"The love with which Pope Emeritus Benedict XVI gave his life in service to the Church was a blessing for the Augustinians and for the Church," then-Bishop Robert Prevost of Chiclayo wrote in 2022, shortly after Benedict's passing.[38] "His intellectual gifts as well as his authentic humanity continue to be a source of inspiration for many," said Prevost, "and now, after so many years of service, the words of Saint Augustine are now also Benedict's: 'This is the eternal life for which we pine. Enter into the joy of your Lord.' (*Confessions* IX, 10)." None of that is to say one should expect to see Leo XIV govern in anything like the way Benedict XVI governed. It is not to say that Leo will return to policy pursued under Benedict. It is to say that one of the retrievals of the Leonine pontificate will be of specifically Augustinian sensibilities, which somehow also informed the teaching pontificate of Benedict XVI.

The pontificate of Leo XIV, however, will not only retrieve them with a view to teaching, but also to governance. What follows in this chapter will be a consideration of two specific, distinct but closely related ideas: law and the rule of law; the Augustinian anthropology that undergirds and informs Augustinian thinking about the nature and scope of power in any society. The reason for this foray into Saint Augustine's thought on these subjects is twofold. For one thing, Leo has already told us he is an Augustinian in his spiritual and intellectual formation, so understanding something of Saint Augustine's mind will help us understand Leo. For another, Leo will sometimes make the Augustinian underpinnings of his expressed thought explicit, but will always be thinking, speaking, and acting from his fundamentally Augustinian cast of mind, even and especially when he does not make it explicit.

Human nature and power in society: an Augustinian view

"[N]o one is exempted from striving to ensure respect for the dignity of every person," Leo XIV has said, "especially the most frail and vulnerable, from the unborn to the elderly, from the sick to the unemployed, citizens and immigrants alike." Given the context in which he offered those remarks—his speech on 16 May 2025, to ambassadors accredited to the Holy See— one may be forgiven for hearing them as having been given primarily *ad extra*. There is a real and powerfully significant sense, however, in which one may and indeed ought to take them as directed subtly but unmistakably also to the worldwide body of Christians, the faithful and their pastors. "For her part," Pope Leo told diplomats accredited to the Holy See, "the Church can never be exempted from speaking the truth about humanity and the world, resorting whenever necessary to blunt language that may initially create misunderstanding."

"Yet truth can never be separated from charity," Leo said— in his very next sentence to the diplomats—showing himself already about the work of charity that presumes good will and spares no pain to overcome precisely the initial mis- understanding such necessary bluntness shall from time to time engender, "which always has at its root a concern for the life and well-being of every man and woman." For an Augustinian, the stakes of communication could not possibly be higher. The souls of men and women are at stake every time anyone speaks. Having the facts to hand—having even knowledge of the truth—is not sufficient even when it is necessary. "Without charity," Saint Augustine wrote in Book IX of his *City of God*, "knowledge does no good, but inflates a man or magnifies him with an empty windiness." Augustine went on to say that knowledge without charity is the property of demons.[39]

Charity, it is important to keep in mind, is not for either Leo or Saint Augustine the rough equivalent of altruistic giving. In the generally Christian and specifically Augustinian register, charity is the perfect and perfectly selfless, self-subsistent love that not only is of God, but is God, in which everything that is participates according to its nature. According to our nature, we humans participate willingly in God's charity, or else we do not. We can choose against God, but we cannot choose against God and hope to be happy. Our every choice and indeed our every breath and heartbeat is somehow seeking God, who made us.

Citizen and stranger

"My own story is that of a citizen," Leo XIV went on to say in his next sentence to the diplomats. "Citizen" is a term crackling with Augustinian incident. "There is a city of God," Augustine wrote in Book XI of *City of God*, "and its Founder has inspired us with a love which makes us covet its citizenship." This is the desire of perfect friendship with God and all our fellows in happy eternity, a desire that lives in the human heart. Baptism is the efficacious sign and promise of citizenship in that city. There is also an "earthly city"—a *civitas terrena* or *terriugena*—founded not on friendship but on fratricide, when Cain slew Abel.

According to a popular misconception, the City of God simply is the Church on Earth and the Earthly City simply is the prevailing political order. According to Saint Augustine's view of things, the matter is more complicated than that. The City of God is on pilgrimage in the world, living secretly and by faith. The Church visible is indeed the sign of that City's pilgrim presence, but there is no single political society—not even Rome—that is simply the Earthly City. Political orders come and go. Political societies form—or are formed—they develop, change, decline, decay, pass away, are replaced and supplanted. Christians in Saint Augustine's day faced a charge not entirely unresembling one levied against Christians and Christianity in our own: That Christian religion is incapable of sustaining the morals of a republic. In Augustine's day, it was the Roman republic, and Roman imperial order as it appeared in the early days of the fifth century AD.[40] There is a real sense in which Saint Augustine's whole project in his *City of God* was to refute that idea and propose an alternative understanding based, however, on a careful and thorough appreciation of Roman history, from which he was able to articulate a general theory of order.

None of the foregoing is to say that Pope Leo XIV should have been thinking of all that history when he made his remark—not exactly, not explicitly or particularly—but it is to note how much heft of spiritual, intellectual, and political history there is in being Augustinian. The weft and warp of history are the work of God through human hands. Having a fellow in the papacy, who shares in the Augustinian cast of mind—the *forma mentis*—is no small thing. Anyone willing or able to see the work of God in human affairs may take it as providential, while others must see it at least as a powerfully significant coincidence. In any case and for everyone, it will take time and effort to get used to it.

Leo in that 16 May 2025 address also called himself, "the descendant of immigrants, who in [his] turn chose to emigrate." Leo then broadened his discourse. "All of us, in the course of our lives, can find ourselves healthy or sick, employed or unemployed, living in our native land or in a foreign country, yet our dignity always remains unchanged," Leo said, "it is the dignity of a creature willed and loved by God." In those lines, we may discern and perhaps discover another Augustinian leitmotiv

of Augustinian spirituality, anthropology, and ecclesiology—
a keystone concept of Saint Augustine's thought, in other
words—i.e., human being as a being in motion, exiled from
our true eternal home in the celestial Jerusalem and existen-
tially either mostly on the way there as pilgrims or else mostly
wandering about as vagabonds, but always priceless in God's
eyes, who always desires us to come safe home.[41]

Augustinian optimism

Even among Christians, Saint Augustine of Hippo is sometimes
mistaken for a fellow with a dim view of human nature. He
gets his bad rap, when he gets it, owing largely to his relentless
insistence on the perduring effects of what Christians call
"Original Sin"—at its most basic level the acknowledgment of
human brokenness and tendency to ruin, of a piece with the
sense of the world as somehow, even if only ever so slightly, out
of sorts—which we cannot really escape in this life. In popular
treatments of Saint Augustine's thought, one will encounter
claims to the effect that he took a "negative" view of human
sexuality, say, or a "pessimistic" view of human nature. Though
few readers who really engage with Saint Augustine long persist
in such misconceptions, it is not surprising that he should have
the reputation he has. Saint Augustine is adamant about the
ineluctable presence of concupiscence—inordinate desire—in
the human soul wounded by sin and awaiting perfect healing in
eternity, utterly dependent upon God's grace to attain it.

Readers of Saint Augustine who do come to conclude he
has a dim view of human nature often miss his overarching
rhetorical operation, which is in service of his anthropology
and ultimately of his soteriology. That is to say, Saint Augustine's
rhetoric is in service of his thinking about the kind of creature
human being is and the kind of saviour God sent to the human
race, hence his thinking about the dignity of God's creation and
the greatness of God's saving work in history. Said simply and

in short, Saint Augustine makes no bones about how bad things have got—in our souls, hence in our affairs—precisely so he can bring into focus and relief how very good they will be and in fact already are. The world, after all, is fallen and awaiting the fullness of its redemption. The only true and lasting victory over sin and death belongs to Christ, Our Lord.

In a world such as ours, especially at present, with distrust of institutions and a strange sense of political messianism simultaneously on the rise, a healthy dose of Augustinian optimism—call it hard-nosed optimism—is a reminder all of us are imperfect even in the best of times. When it comes to citizenship—whether of heaven somehow mysteriously in and through the Church, or of the political societies in which we participate while we are yet in time and subject to the round of history—we mostly muddle. If we pause to think of it for just a moment, we see that most of citizenship is muddling. We have no real choice, if we would fulfil our duties to ourselves, our families, our fellows, but to be about the mostly muddling work. The contribution Catholics have to make, today as in Augustine's day, is one of example. We will not get another.

This Augustinian understanding of human nature and the condition of human being in the world may well inform Pope Leo XIV's direction of Vatican and Church policy vis-à-vis the phenomenon of migration, for example. In fact, his remark of his own status as citizen and immigrant-emigrant followed words that were a stark reminder of common duty to our fellows, each according to his station and role in society. "[N]o one is exempted from striving to ensure respect for the dignity of every person," Leo told the gathered diplomats, "especially the most frail and vulnerable, from the unborn to the elderly, from the sick to the unemployed, citizens and immigrants alike." That is also a powerful interpretative key to his rhetoric, hence to his thinking in general. In short, we may reasonably expect an Augustinian anthropological framework—Saint Augustine's view of human nature, being, and condition in the world—to inform the mind of the Augustinian pope not only in matters of particular policy but generally, across the whole sweep of his thought and action in government, even and especially when it is not explicit.

In very broad strokes, Saint Augustine's view has it that the role of law—hence of the legislator—is to help establish and maintain the order necessary for people in society to achieve their temporal and spiritual purposes: concord in this life and happiness in the next. The Church, for Saint Augustine, is in the world as the carrier of souls to their—to our—eternal homeland, but she is not therefore perfectly preserved from the vicissitudes of human nature while she is underway. For the Church to be herself, her "best self" we might say, she must have order in her own affairs, and good order will account for the frailties and indeed the brokenness of those who participate in it, as well as for their excellences. The Church, in other words, needs to have her own house in order if she is to be a credible, effective witness in the world. Rule of law is important for the Church, in other words, for the very straightforward reason that the Church is a society and one that must lead by example if she is to lead at all.

Pope Leo XIV, in short, is an Augustinian. He has spoken several times since his election, of the great Bishop and Doctor of the Church, whose Rule and example together constitute the charism of community and faith-seeking-understanding, which have not only signed but formed the pope's character and personality. We have seen how anyone seeking to understand the significance of having such an Augustinian on Peter's throne, must first understand Saint Augustine of Hippo's thinking about human nature. It is also owing to Leo's Augustinian formation, that he brings to the papal office a deep sense of history and of the Church's pilgrim place in it. That sense, we shall begin to see shortly, has also informed his choice of regnal name.

Chapter 5

A Lion of springtime

There was a story that made the rounds in Rome in the days following the conclave that elected Pope Leo XIV, according to which one senior churchman would have said to another at table, just after Leo's election: *Abbiamo avuto un Francesco che parlava coi lupi, e ora abbiamo un Leone che gli da la caccia*—"We had a Francis who talked with the wolves, and now we have a Leo who hunts them." The joke is a typically Italian play on the name of Francis and his sainted namesake of Assisi (about whose prodigious conversion of an old, wizened wolf a golden legend is still told to Italian children) and on Leo, which is Latin for lion. The story is apocryphal and quite possibly cut from whole cloth. So far as I have been able to tell, no one has sourced it. *Se non è vero, è ben trovato*, as the Italians say—literally, "If it isn't true, it is well found"—the functional equivalent of the homespun English, "If it ain't true, it oughtta be." Whether Leo will show himself a hunter of wolves remains to be seen, but he has already given a good deal in the way of an explanation for his choice.

"I chose to take the name Leo XIV," he told the cardinals gathered in the New Synod Hall on 10 May 2025, the Saturday after his election. "There are different reasons for this," Leo said, "but mainly because Pope Leo XIII, in his historic encyclical, *Rerum novarum*, addressed the social question in the context of the first great industrial revolution." Leo went on to say that in the present day as well, "[T]he Church offers to everyone the treasury of her social teaching," this time, "in response to another industrial revolution and to developments in the field of artificial intelligence that pose new challenges for the defence of human dignity, justice and labour." That explanation was very revealing, it turns out.

The Church's social doctrine in the modern era began with Leo XIII in *Rerum novarum*, a seminal work that dealt with issues of its day but was not merely of its time. *Rerum novarum*, which carried "on capital and labour" as its subtitle, may have been the first word of the Church's highest teaching authority at a moment of truly seismic upheaval in human affairs, but it was not the last. *Rerum novarum*'s great genius was in its recovery of the anthropological question as the focus of thought, social action, and political life. Leo sees the world not on the cusp of another such revolution, but already in the throes of it, and he has already begun to frame the challenge in anthropological terms.

"[T]here are the challenges that call into question respect for the dignity of the human person," Leo told the bishops of Italy in a speech on 17 June 2025. "Artificial intelligence, biotechnologies, data economy and social media are profoundly transforming our perception and our experience of life," he continued. Leo noted how human dignity—even human nature itself—is at risk of being eclipsed or forgotten, "substituted by functions, automatism, simulations," he said.

"But the person is not a system of algorithms," Leo continued, "he or she is a creature, relationship, mystery." Leo asked the bishops of Italy to develop "the [Church's] anthropological vision as an essential tool of pastoral discernment." He said ethics is reduced to a mere code and faith itself risks disembodiment when they are made to go without animated "reflection on the human being – in its corporeality, its vulnerability, its thirst for the infinite and capacity for bonding."

"You have the opportunity," Pope Leo XIV told participants in the annual gathering of the *Centesimus annus pro Pontifice* group (which took its name and inspiration from the 1991 encyclical letter of Pope St. John Paul II marking the hundredth anniversary of *Rerum novarum*'s promulgation), also on 17 May

2025, "to show that the Church's social doctrine, with its specific anthropological approach, seeks to encourage genuine engagement with social issues." Leo went on to say that the Church's social doctrine "does not claim to possess a monopoly on truth, either in its analysis of problems or its proposal of concrete solutions," but offers a way of thinking about social problems rooted in the changeless reality of human nature. "Where social questions are concerned," Leo said, "knowing how best to approach them is more important than providing immediate responses to why things happen or how to deal with them."

Pope Leo XIV's focus on the anthropological—on human nature, hence the Church's "expert[ise] in humanity" as Pope St. Paul VI put it in his landmark address to the United Nations on 4 October 1965—is evidently nothing new. Leo, however, brings something to the conversation we have not seen in some time: a pope who is a missionary pastor and governor, whose fundamental outlooked is shaped, moulded, and infused with an Augustinian spirituality and intellectual formation. Leo will see the historical moment within an arc of history, and will see the arc of history in the peculiar historical moment. The cardinals' choice of this particular fellow was startling, but perhaps it ought not have been surprising.

Most of the media coverage heading into the conclave that elected Leo XIV, it is fair to say, focused heavily—indeed almost exclusively—on supposed divisions in the College of Cardinals along ideological lines. The old conservative/liberal divide typified by debates over "tradition"—whether "values conservatism" or Latin liturgy or the like—and progressive darlings like women in clerical roles or gay marriage. "[T]he debates of the second half of the twentieth century," as Charles Collins succinctly and astutely noted in a 2 May 2025 news analysis for *Crux*. "The first part of the twenty-first century sees a society questioning what it means to be human," Collins wrote, "with 'post-humanism' being pushed by the leaders of many technology firms,[42]" and the Lords of Big Tech touting the emergence of AI "virtual friends" to supply the need for human companionship we all have, the absence of which—paradoxically perhaps—is felt more keenly than ever in our world of virtual connections.

Technological eclipse

The Augustinian cannot fail to blanch at the notion of friendship's eclipse, especially at the prospect of friendship's eclipse by technology. Saint Augustine is widely known as the *Doctor gratiae*—the "Doctor of Grace" and sometimes as the *Doctor caritatis*, the "Doctor of Charity" (though St. Francis de Sales, patron of writers and journalists, it happens, has that title since 1877)—but he may well have come to be known as the *Doctor amicitiae*—the "Doctor of Friendship"—owing to his praise of that fundamental and imprescindible human relation, so utterly necessary for human flourishing. Of an unnamed friend who died suddenly, Saint Augustine famously wrote in Book IV of his *Confessions*: "I felt that my soul and my own friend's soul were but one soul in two bodies; and, so truly, life was a horror to me because I would not live as half-myself."

"So it happened," Saint Augustine continued, "that I feared to die, lest he should die wholly, whom I had so greatly loved." Saint Augustine also wrote warnings about the dangers and pitfalls of friendship that forms around ungodly interest and tends to feed rather than to discipline or attenuate our appetites for good things; around things loved either for their own sake when they ought to be merely useful, or loved out of proportion with their goodness; or even with persons for the sake of their very wickedness—their lack of wholesomeness—so great is our desire and indeed our need of friendship. We will not only accept a weak and unbecoming simulacrum of friendship, Saint Augustine knew, but even seek and chase counterfeits when we despair of the genuine article.

In recent decades and centuries especially, some readers of Saint Augustine have discovered what they take to be (or to

72

present as) a fairly dismal view of corporeality in general and of the human body—our embodiment—in particular, ostensibly owing often to the alacrity with which Saint Augustine exposes everything in the created order to the caustic process of critical examination in the light of faith. If Saint Augustine's *Confessions* teach us anything at all, it must be that creation is good—creation praises God willy-nilly—and that human nature's very excellence makes all creation very good, indeed, and that human nature is corporal and corporate. We are made for friendship with God, who after all took on human flesh to save us.

That is not nothing.

It is a commonplace of Christian discourse to speak of the Church as the Body of Christ. It is an expression full of mystery and indeed expressing a mystical reality. It is also mere prosaic description of what the Church is. Leo XIV—the Augustinian pope—sees the mystical reality in the prose and sees the prose in the mystical reality, and he draws the real, practical, nuts-and-bolts conclusions. "No-one can prevent you from being close to the people, sharing life, walking with the last, serving the poor," Leo told the Italian bishops. "No one can prevent you from proclaiming the Gospel," he said, "and it is the Gospel that we are invited to bring, because it is this that everyone, ourselves first, need in order to live well and to be happy."

Pope Leo XIV invited the Italian bishops to see that the laity, "nourished with the Word of God and formed in the social doctrine of the Church," should be, "agents of evangelisation in the workplace, in schools, in hospitals, in social and cultural environments, in the economy, and in politics." Leo XIV, in short, is calling not for revolution, nor for restoration, but for recovery of the Augustinian ethos that permeates the Church, running at present in secret rivulets and often—more often than we realize—hiding in plain sight. Celebrating a newly promulgated Mass for the Care of Creation on 9 July 2025 in the *Borgo Laudato Si'* at Castel Gandolfo, Pope Leo invoked his spiritual father. "Saint Augustine," Leo said, "in the last pages of his *Confessions*, brought together creation and humanity in a cosmic hymn of praise: Lord, 'your works praise you, that we may love you; may we love you, that your works may praise you' (XIII.xxxiii.48)."

"May this be the harmony that we spread throughout the world," Leo concluded, the remark telling also of the way in which Pope Leo XIV intends to advance the work of his immediate predecessor, Pope Francis. Leo, it happens, described the new Mass for the Care of Creation as "the fruit of the work of several Dicasteries of the Holy See," a nod to the institutional effort the new Mass represented, hence to the individuals who brought the work to fruition. Celebrating in the *Borgo Laudato Si'* also suggested the importance of community in the work of Christian witness. *Laudato Si'*, the great encyclical of the Francis pontificate, carried the subtitle: On care for our common home. There is an emerging Leonine sensibility of threats to our common home from forces subtly and constantly at work in and on human society.

Worse (and also better)

One of the most troubling aspects of contemporary life is the subtraction of public space—common space—in the real world. If you walk through a municipal park, you may find pop-up shops in semi-permanent kiosks selling all sorts of wares. Design-forward benches and railings and other such accoutrement in gardens and along the streets of gentrifying neighbourhoods discourage loiterers from resting their weary limbs too long and keep rough sleepers from finding repose. In almost any recently redesigned airport, you'll find you have to run a gauntlet of commercial vendors before you come to a place where you can just sit down—if you ever come to one at all—and even there you may be encouraged (if you are not required) to part with some of your money in exchange for creature comforts. The phenomenon is not universal—not yet—but it is perceptible to the naked eye. It is increasingly difficult to credit the idea that the phenomenon is a mere natural or organic expression of human transactions in general.

The subtraction of public space appears to be very much by design, a feature rather than a bug in the "system" of our civilization. Paradoxically, perhaps, there is also less and less space in which private conversations can unfold. In the pervasive digital space that is a peculiar characteristic of twenty-first-century life, everything is immediately before everyone, all the time. "Pic, or it didn't happen!" has become the default setting of the digital age. A mere list of the scandals involving ill-considered remarks or injudicious oversharing on social media in the last ten years would fill more than one weighty volume.

It was not ever thus.

Thirty years ago, if I may offer a cheeky example (and date myself), snarky teenagers with dark humour and little in the way of a social filter could gather in the garage or basement of a friend's house or in a park or a field or in a local coffee shop to crack wise. Photographic evidence of adolescent hijinks existed on film, mostly in stills, when it existed at all. Usually, it didn't—a fact for which Gen-Xers frequently give sincere thanks, ironically, through internet memes and shorts (often to powerful comic effect). When such evidence did exist, it was tucked in a drawer or kept in a chest that lived forgotten in a closet or attic.

Today, even pre-adolescent children live online. Parents, schoolteachers, administrators, and counsellors have raised the alarm over the baleful effects of perpetually online existence. Adolescents—boys and girls, equally though differently—experience constant stimulation not entirely unresembling, on a neurochemical level, the stress of soldiers in sustained contact with the enemy. Attention spans shrink and critical faculties atrophy (or hardly develop). Young people not only fail to develop authentic and meaningful relationships through careful and gradual self-disclosure and cultivation of vulnerability, but often struggle to talk with one another at all.

The paradoxical reduction of space for human intimacy proceeds apace with the commercialisation of public spaces. Both contribute to the profound sense of disorientation characteristic of contemporary life. The existence of both public and private space is increasingly threatened. The senses—the meaning, scope, direction, and purpose—of each are increasingly obscure.

Attention deficit

Fr. Robert Prevost OSA trenchantly addressed this phenomenon in an intervention he made as a Father—or full member—of the XIII Ordinary General Assembly of the Synod of Bishops in 2012, to which the Union of Superiors General elected him. Then-Fr. Prevost identified the challenge facing those responsible for sharing the Gospel—all the baptised, in other words, each according to station—as essentially one of rhetoric. "Church fathers," he said in his 2012 address to the Synod Fathers, "were great preachers because they were first great rhetoricians." He explained how the success of their preaching owed, in human terms, to their understanding of the socio-cultural realities of the people to whom they preached. "In other words," Prevost said, "their evangelising was successful in great part because they understood the foundations of social communication appropriate to the world in which they lived."

"Consequently," Prevost continued, "they understood with enormous precision the techniques through which popular religious and ethical imaginations of their day were manipulated by the centres of secular power in that world." In an interview[43] with CNS during that same Synod Assembly, Prevost said he had chosen to make mention of the Church fathers "because of an Augustinian perspective and I think also a rediscovery that the church has made since the time of the [Vatican] Council [II] with respect to the value that the study of the fathers of the church has." Prevost's interest in the fathers of the Church was neither solely nor even primarily academic. "[W]e are convinced that the fathers of the Church have a great deal to contribute because of a number of parallel or similar circumstances that the church lived in the first centuries and that the church is living today," Prevost said. He also described a tendency, already diffuse in the present of 2012, "to look at the secular world, if you will, what we call the secular world today, for all the answers and a discovery that all the answers are not there[.]"

"[P]eople are really looking for something else," Prevost said, "for understanding life and death, for understanding who we are as human beings, and what our life is all about – that the fathers do indeed have a great deal to say to us." Prevost also noted how one of the major problems in increasingly dire need of address is that of captivating an increasingly distracted, disinterested, and desensitised audience. "How are we going to get people to come back and listen?" He asked. It was—in the strict, technical sense of the term—a rhetorical question, i.e., a question of rhetoric. It is a question, the urgency of which has only become more apparent in the intervening years.

How the Church communicates

Social media have a role to play in the evangelising work of the Church and of baptised Christians because social media are part of the cultural environment in which we all live and operate, for good and for ill. Indeed, one of the most important *nova* of the new Leonine era into which the world has come, is that Pope Leo XIV is the first man to come into Peter's see with an established social media presence. "I personally put some things up once in a while on Facebook," then-Fr Prevost explained in the 2012 CNS interview. He went on to note his amazement "at the very quick response" he would receive from around the world. He understood that part of the interest in his social media activity came "because there are Augustinians and lay people connected with the Augustinian order" who follow his Facebook page.

"I'll put a little piece of news up there, an invitation, a little reflection at times," he said, "and that is a way of reaching people." Pope Leo XIV is the first worldwide leader of the Catholic Church to have his own personal social media presence that predates his institutional leadership role at the global level. That is new, indeed. It offers both a key to understanding his public thinking about the challenges of communication and a reason to be interested in what he has to say, regardless of whether one is Catholic.

It is difficult to overstate the significance of having an internet-literate man in the See of Peter. Pope Francis, by contrast, often relied on his secretaries to photograph or scan his handwritten notes and send them to correspondents via email. Fr. James Martin SJ, a Jesuit priest from the United States active in ministry to LGBTQ Catholics (no stranger to controversy), told Ross Douthat of *The New York Times* he would "send [Francis] more formal notes typed out in Spanish or Italian," while Francis' secretaries "would send me back scanned PDFs of his handwritten note, which they would have to transcribe or transliterate because it was this tiny little handwriting." Culture warriors on every side of the lines running through both Church and society have a take on Francis' encouragement of Martin's controversial approach to LGBTQ ministry. For this old Vatican hand, the major takeaway from that 24 April 2025 interview with Douthat in the NYT[44] was Martin's description of the way Francis corresponded with him. We know that Pope Leo XIV keeps in touch with friends and family via text message and email. There is a great photograph of Leo celebrating the birthday of Fr. Alejandro Moral OSA—his successor as prior general and an old friend—enjoying something or other on a cell phone screen in the company of his Augustinian confrères. This is a generational difference, to be sure, but it is one that will have powerful repercussions for the way Pope Leo XIV governs the Church.[45]

More than a decade before he took a senior curial position and more than a dozen years before he became pope, Robert Prevost was already thinking about how the Church communicates. He has been thinking about communications since before he took the habit of his Order of Saint Augustine. Indeed, from a very tender age—to hear Leo himself tell it—he has been thinking about the nexus of communion and communication, *communio* and *communicatio*. "Around age six," Leo told an international group of youngsters gathered in the Paul VI Hall in the Vatican on 3 July 2025, for a special audience during their Vatican-sponsored summer camp, "I was also an altar server in my parish. Before going to school—it was a parish school—we would attend 06:30 Mass. Mom always woke us up saying, 'Let's go to Mass'."

Leo told his audience—the sons and daughters of Vatican employees, and a large contingent of Ukrainian children—that serving at Mass was something he truly enjoyed. "From an early age, I was taught that Jesus is always near, that He is your best friend, and Mass was a way to find that friend, to be with Jesus — even before my First Communion." Leo recalled learning the Latin responses an altar server had to know in those days, as well. "We had to learn Latin for Mass, but then it changed to English for me since I was born and raised in the U.S."

"What mattered wasn't the language of the celebration," Pope Leo XIV told the children, "but the experience of being with other kids serving Mass, the friendship, and that closeness to Jesus in the Church. It was always something beautiful." Leo's point was of the sort children, especially, are prepared to grasp: that sharing experiences, duties, burdens—including the burden of rising earlier than one may otherwise wish—joys and trials, is the very stuff of human relationship, which takes us out of ourselves and makes us part of something greater.[46] Human being is made in the image and after the likeness of God, which is to say, in constitutive conversation with the divine author of our common nature. To be in conversation—to communicate, which literally says "to make common"—is just what we are made to do.

It is not that the point has at once a personal and a social application. It is rather one and the same point, with personal and social valences. Human being is personal and social, social and personal. The personal and the social are functions of one another, to say it mathematically—a point Pope Leo XIV, whose undergraduate degree from the Augustinians' Villanova University just a little north and west of Philadelphia, PA in the United States just happened to be in mathematics, would perhaps appreciate—always somehow acting on one another. In a word, the point is anthropological. Our understanding of what constitutes communication, in other words, is too narrow.

The Catholic Church has preserved the sense of communication-as-sharing in her technical language. To "communicate" may mean, for example, to partake of the Sacrament of Holy Communion. The hifalutin' *communicatio in sacris* is a term referring to the sharing of sacred things and more specifically of Sacraments. Broadly, then, communication is an essential human activity in which we are always somehow engaged, even if we do not quite know it. Fostering and nurturing spaces in which we may express and disclose ourselves to ourselves is likewise essential, necessary, and imprescindible. As Pope Leo XIV put it to the summer camp children, "Experiences like this—meeting people from different countries, lands, languages, with so many differences between us—are very important." Leo encouraged his guests to welcome and take up, with gusto, "the experience of encounter, of meeting one another, of mutual respect, and learning to be friends with one another."

Leo XIV and the "culture of encounter"

"Help us," Pope Leo XIV prayed from the *loggia* above St. Peter's Basilica on the afternoon of his election, "one and all, to build bridges through dialogue and encounter, joining together as one people, always at peace." It was a nod to Pope Francis, but it would be a mistake to take it as a sop. Leo's concern for the urgently needful work of fostering human community is manifest. "It is still possible," he told the participants in a charity soccer match to benefit Rome's Bambino Gesù children's hospital on 16 July 2025, "it is always possible to encounter one another, even in a time of divisions, bombs, and wars."

Pope Francis frequently called for a "culture of encounter" to answer the crisis of human alienation. Some of Francis' most eloquent writing was on just this subject, as were some of the most memorable passages from his homilies and speeches. "[I]t is important to be ready for encounter," Francis said to thousands of pilgrim faithful gathered in St. Peter's Square on 15 May 2013 to celebrate the vigil of Pentecost, Francis' first recorded use of the term as pope.[47] "Because faith is an encounter with Jesus," Francis said, "and we must do what Jesus does: encounter others. We live in a culture of conflict, a culture of fragmentation, a culture in which I throw away what is of no use to me, a throwaway culture."

The appearance of "throwaway culture" in those remarks is also noteworthy.[48] It is fair to say that "throwaway culture" as a term has garnered wide interest. Articles have appeared in Catholic and mainstream secular publications—not all of them perfectly sharing or even friendly to Christianity—discussing and exploring not only Pope Francis' use of the term but the ideas that inform it. Whether "throwaway culture" will gain currency or even real traction far beyond the confines of Catholic and broadly Christian discourse, however, remains to be seen. Regardless of the term's success or failure in the lexicon of public discourse, the thing it names is real, really pernicious, and ubiquitous.[49]

The rise of AI, in the vanguard of technological changes disrupting human affairs on a scale not seen since the industrial revolution, frequently presents as a driver of both alienation and the throwaway culture. Pope Leo XIV, who identified the rise of AI as a revolutionary disruptive force in civilization almost on Day One of his pontificate and marked it as a key reason for his choice of regnal name, also sees the enormous potential of emerging technologies to serve the common good. "AI," Leo wrote in a Message he sent to experts and tech executives in Rome and at the Vatican for an international conference on AI, Ethics and the Future of Corporate Governance over two days, 19 – 20 June 2025, "especially Generative AI, has opened new horizons on many different levels, including enhancing research in healthcare and scientific discovery." Leo noted as well, how the rise of AI "also raises troubling questions on its possible repercussions on humanity's openness to truth and beauty, on our distinctive ability to grasp and process reality."

"Acknowledging and respecting what is uniquely characteristic of the human person is essential to the discussion of any adequate ethical framework for the governance of AI," Leo wrote. The people taking part in the conference, including the Catholics both institutional and individual, were among the social, cultural, and civilizational elite of the present day. The 2025 Rome Conference on AI was the second iteration of the gathering, which began under Pope Francis. The text of the Message eventually delivered above Pope Leo XIV's signature was in the works before the change in papal leadership. It would be a mistake to read too deeply into the text for specific insights into Leo XIV's thinking about AI or the underlying anthropological crisis the rise of AI at once instances and engenders.

Here, again, Leo's specific audience was at least as important as the words of the Message, which—journalists noted—was written in English. Often enough in the Vatican, such and similar statements and documents have been released in Italian— usually the language of composition—even when the working language of the participants was English (or occasionally French). Occasionally, significant lower-level documents like official statements from the Holy See's diplomatic representatives to the United Nations in New York or Geneva, will be composed and released in either English or French (or both, since both are official working languages at the UN), but Italians in high places within the Vatican's complex of communications and media outfits will wait for the "original" Italian to be available internally before distributing the documents. One effect of the Leonine pontificate may well prove therefore to be a cultural shift away from the Italo-centric cultural default within the Vatican communications apparatus.

In any case, Pope Leo XIV's Message this time was addressed directly to executives and board members from companies like OpenAI, AI21, Google, Anthropic, and Palantir. There were leading high-tech manufacturing firms represented, as well, like Lumentum, while several speakers covered roles in academia as well as business. There were lawyers, members of the United Nations' AI Committee, and career researchers among the participants. "Your presence," Leo wrote to them, "attests to the urgent need for serious reflection and ongoing discussion on the inherently ethical dimension of AI, as well as its responsible governance." Leo went on to express his pleasure "that the second day of the Conference will take place in the Apostolic Palace." Leo said the hosting of Day Two was "a clear indication of the Church's desire to participate in these discussions that directly affect the present and future of our human family."

From the personal to the institutional— continuities and discontinuities

One may discern a point of community or continuity uniting Pope Leo XIV and Pope Francis, albeit with significant differences in style, substance, and general approach. In an 11 April 2024 address to participants in the plenary assembly of the Pontifical Academy for Social Sciences, to mark the 30th anniversary of the Academy's founding, Francis discussed the rise of AI, listing it among the most urgent challenges of the day. "I am thinking," he said, "of technology and its implications for research and for fields such as medicine and ecological transition," specifically mentioning, "communications and the development of artificial intelligence (a great challenge indeed!), as well as the need to devise new economic models." There is an institutional response—a role for institutions including the Church and her ancillary and subsidiary institutions, like the Pontifical Academy of Social Sciences, each according to its ability and mission-profile—which any leader must carefully calibrate.

In three dense paragraphs in that same speech, Pope Francis also articulated the baleful effects of throwaway culture and broadly outlined the spiritual wherewithal to resist it. "The throwaway culture, in effect, has no borders," Francis said. "There are those who presume to be able to establish, on the basis of utilitarian and functional criteria, when a life has value and is worth being lived." Francis was not speaking of theoretical possibilities or far-off nightmare scenarios of dystopian fiction. Francis was speaking of present-day realities and real-life prospects in political societies across the developed and broadly Western world, from euthanasia and assisted suicide to the eugenic prenatal termination of persons who return positive results on screening tests for genetic disorders, and a host of other similar and related practices.[50]

Pope Leo XIV, in his explanation of his choice of regnal name, his Message to the AI conference, his remarks to the bishops of Italy and those to the Inter Parliamentary Union, and elsewhere, has practiced evident message-discipline, while also tailoring his words to his specific audience. He has also sought to encourage and empower his hearers in their respective areas of competence and fields of endeavour. He has done so primarily within specific institutional contexts. Leo has begun to show himself, in short, an institutionalist by character and temperament. That is not to say, however, that he sees institutions as the primary actors in human affairs.

"History and practical experience have taught us that authentic peace takes shape from the ground up," Pope Leo XIV told the members of the Movements and Associations of the "Arena of Peace"—a Verona-based initiative launched by Pope Francis in 2024—who were gathered in the Clementine Hall of the Apostolic Palace in the Vatican on 30 May 2025,

Newly elected Pope Leo XIV gestures on the main central loggia balcony of the St Peter's Basilica. A moderate who was close to Pope Francis and spent years as a missionary in Peru, he becomes the Catholic Church's 267th pontiff, taking the papal name Leo XIV.

Pope Leo XIV leads the Pro Ecclesia Mass in the Sistine Chapel, on 9 May 2025 in the Vatican, using the pastoral staff of Benedict XVI.

Pope Leo XIV greets pilgrims gathered in St Peter's Square for the Angelus prayer and reflects on Christian unity, conversion, and the witness of martyrdom that binds the Church in a deep and often hidden communion.

Pope Leo XIV delivers his blessing during the Holy Mass on the Solemnity of Saints Peter and Paul at St. Peter's Basilica in the Vatican. The Mass included the blessing and imposition of the pallium on 54 new Metropolitan Archbishops.

Pope Leo XIV ordains 32 new priests during a Mass for the ordination of new priests in St. Peter's Basilica on the Solemnity of the Sacred Heart of Jesus on 27 June 2025 in Vatican City.

Pope Leo XIV waves to the faithful and pilgrims during his weekly general audience at St. Peter's Square.

(Above) View of St. Peter's Square with a crowd of faithful during the Holy Mass celebrated by Pope Leo XIV on the occasion of the Jubilee of Families, Children, Grandparents, and the Elderly. (Below) Pope Francis receives Bishop Robert Francis Prevost in audience.

(Above) Cardinal Prevost is seen during a Pro Eligendo Romano Pontifice Mass ahead of the Conclave, in which he and the other cardinal electors are called to elect a new Pope. (Below) Pope Leo XIV receives Daughters of Divine Charity, Sisters of the Order of Saint Basil the Great, Augustinian Sisters of Amparo, and Franciscan Sisters of the Sacred Heart during an audience at the Apostolic Palace in June 2025.

The then–Bishop Robert Prevost often journeyed on horseback to reach the faithful in rural Peru.

Pope Leo XIV greets a child during his weekly general audience at St. Peter's Square in June 2025 in Vatican City.

(Above) Crowds of people in the square waiting for the new Pope. (Right) Pope Leo XIV addresses the crowd from the window of the apostolic palace overlooking St. Peter's square during the Angelus prayer in The Vatican on 29 June 2025.

"beginning with places, communities and local institutions, and by listening to what they have to tell us." Leo went on to say, "If you want peace, prepare institutions of peace," a telling riff on Pope St. Paul VI's famous dictum.[51] "Increasingly," Pope Leo XIV said, "we realize that this cannot simply involve political institutions, whether national or international, but requires all institutions – educational, economic and social." Leo then noted how Pope Francis' encyclical letter, *Fratelli tutti*, "frequently spoke of the need to pass from 'I' to 'we', in a spirit of solidarity that needs to find institutional expression." Whether Pope Leo XIV will be able to repair the institutions of the Church and foster new ones through a recovery of the Church's own self-confidence as an expert in humanity deserving of the world's attention, remains to be seen.

Interlude

The State of the Vatican (and the state of the Church)

If you read the newspapers before the conclave that elected Pope Leo XIV, you might have got the impression the Catholic Church had undergone radical but incomplete change under Pope Francis, and that the conclave was shaping up to be a referendum on the changes Francis had wrought. If one credited the dominant narrative heading into the conclave, Francis had been a maverick visionary reformer who set a new course of openness to all sorts of people on the "existential peripheries" of the Church and of society, from LGBTQ people to the divorced and civilly remarried, to those seeking changes to prevailing Church discipline regarding the admission of married men to the priesthood, to those desiring a place for women in ordained ministry, and beyond. The pontificate of Francis had refocused attention on the poor and downtrodden—a "poor Church for the poor" in Francis' words—especially though by no means exclusively for migrants and refugees. There was some truth to all that.

Indeed, the pontificate of Francis had been different—very different—but it was not revolutionary, not exactly, certainly not in the usual sense. If *Hagan lio!* had been one rallying cry of his pontificate, *Todos! Todos! Todos!*—"Everyone! Everyone! Everyone!"—had been the other. "In the Church," Francis had told young people gathered in Lisbon, Portugal, on 3 August 2023 for the welcome ceremony of the XXXVII World Youth Day, "no one is left out or left over. There is room for everyone, just the way we are." Only, there was a great deal of evidence to suggest the answer Francis proffered did not fit the question most people—especially young people—had regarding the Catholic faith and the Catholic Church. Young people, especially though not exclusively, were not so much concerned with the question whether there was space for them in the Church, as they were with the question whether the Church—increasingly, whether any institution—was worth their while.[52]

"Listen to Jesus," Francis had told young people in Lisbon. "Otherwise," he said, "even if we set out with good intentions along paths that seem to be of love, in the end those paths will be seen as selfishness disguised as love." That was the beginning, at least, of an answer to their deeper question. During the Francis pontificate, however, a series of scandals involving sexual abuse and cover-up, financial mismanagement and malfeasance, and extreme heavy-handedness in governance often on flimsy evidence, had emerged at a time of increasing diffidence toward institutions in general, conspiring to make the Church appear like any other institution. The conclave, therefore, was perhaps better understood as a referendum on the way Francis had governed.

It was not, however, a fight over his legacy. For the men who were going to be in the room, for churchmen around the world, and for laity and Church observers around the world, it was difficult to speak of a legacy, at all. The reason for this was not that Pope Francis had tried a programme and failed. The reason was that Francis did not have a programme. "Reform on the go" was what veteran Vatican beat journalist Andrea Gagliarducci called it, basically a trial-and-error process, which was a hallmark of his efforts to reshape not only the Roman Curia, but the modes and orders of the Church broadly considered. His pontificate was—to hear him and his close advisors tell it— one of discernment, a key notion of the Ignatian spirituality in which Francis was formed.

Reform "on the go"

"Discernment," one word, was the answer Pope Francis gave to Fr. Antonio Spadaro SJ, when Spadaro asked Francis—who had been in office a matter of months at the time—to explain his understanding of "the role of service to the universal Church" Francis had been called to play, "in the light of Ignatian spirituality[.]" Francis went on to say, "This discernment takes time. For example, many think that changes and reforms can take place in a short time. I believe that we always need time to lay the foundations for real, effective change." The question for the conclave in May of 2025 was not whether Francis had succeeded, but whether he had really begun.

"This is the time of discernment," Pope Francis told Spadaro, who would go on to become one of Francis' close advisors and principal public interpreters, especially during the first five years of the Francis pontificate. Francis noted how discernment sometimes drives one to do things in a different order, to proceed immediately or in fairly short order, with projects and decisions one originally intended to pursue at a later date. "[T]hat is what has happened to me in recent months," Francis said. It was August 2013.[53] "Discernment in the Lord guides me in my way of governing," Francis said, adding that he was "always wary of decisions made hastily," and "always wary of the first decision, that is, the first thing that comes to my mind if I have to make a decision."

"This is usually the wrong thing," Pope Francis said. "The wisdom of discernment redeems the necessary ambiguity of life and helps us find the most appropriate means," he said, "which do not always coincide with what looks great and strong." By 2016, certain of Francis' senior lieutenants were offering conspicuously erudite explanations for Francis' "reform on the go" *modus procedendi*, including then–Bishop Marcello Semeraro, Secretary of the "C9" Council of Cardinal Advisors created by Francis in 2013 to draft a new Apostolic Constitution for the Roman Curia.

"With graduality," Semeraro said of Francis' curial reform as it was being implemented in 2016, "but without uncertainties." Reforms were coming, piecemeal, sometimes with a step forward and sometimes in another direction. Semeraro noted in his essay for *Il Regno*, how several major pieces of the piecemeal reform Francis was implementing had come *ad experimentum*— on a trial basis—but without the usual three-year or five-year limit on such "experimental" provisions usually given in Vatican legislation. The practical upshot of the indefinite experiments was that no one knew what would change or when. There was no sense of regularity in operations, no confidence in how things were supposed to work, hence a great deal of uncertainty—and the paralysis that comes with it—across the whole curial apparatus.

The curial reform, however, was part and parcel of a larger vision, also emerging. "We may agree," wrote Semeraro in summation of a lengthy and learned rehearsal[54] of the history of curial reforms, especially though not exclusively those from the twentieth century to the present of 2016, "that Francis is not thinking primarily of a reform of ecclesiastical structures, but first and foremost rather of a reform that touches the lives of Christians and is capable of changing them (in this sense, the word conversion also applies)."

Regarding the Roman Curia specifically, however, Semeraro evinced a driving idea of the reform, according to which the Roman Curia should have been considered a mere instrument at the service of the Roman pontiff. The Roman Curia certainly is an instrument, but it is not a mere instrument. In fairness to Semeraro, he was quoting—albeit with approbation—a remark Francesco Cardinal Coccopalmerio, then President of the Pontifical Council for Legislative Texts, had offered to Nicola Gori for *L'Osservatore Romano* during the course of an interview published 24 July 2014. "The Curia," Coccopalmerio said, "is not, nor can it be, a power structure opposed to the pope, because in that case it would make no sense." It would, indeed, make no sense for the Roman Curia—or any Curia—to be erected in opposition to its principal. The Curia most definitely is a power structure, one designed however not to enable the Roman pontiff in the accomplishment of his every whim, but to help him study, craft, and execute the government of the Church.

"The Curia," Coccopalmerio said, "is, rather, only a service structure to assist the Pope and his work of service to the universal Church, the dioceses, the pastors, and the faithful." The "only" in that sentence—*solo* in Italian—was doing a great deal of work. It is one thing to say the Curia is an instrument. It is quite another to say it is a mere instrument. To think the Curia an instrument, the sole purpose of which is to execute the will of the one directing it in each and every particular, is very much another thing entirely.

By late 2017, it was apparent that Pope Francis understood the reform mandate that had come with his election in a manner very different from that of the cardinals who had elected him. In November of 2017, in fact, Spadaro participated in a gathering of "pro-Francis" journalists who met in Madrid for an event billed as the *I Encuentro Internacional de Periodistas 'Pro Papa Francisco'*. The meeting included participants from ten different countries, and produced a "Final Declaration" which blurred the lines between journalism and activism (however laudable the motives).[55] Organizers reported a "reduced" turnout, but Spadaro's remarks were well received.[56]

As reported by Spanish outfit *Religión Digital*, Spadaro in his remarks called Francis' thinking about government, "Open and incomplete," meaning that Francis "[did] not have a plan for the Church," because "he [was] not an ideological pope," but approached leadership as a process "based on the dynamic of trial and error." Francis' approach, "destabilizes those who seek certainties," *Religión Digital* reported Spadaro as saying, because "discernment is not based on human certainties, but on enabling the unfolding of God's will in history." If that really was an accurate encapsulation of Francis' mind, then Francis would have conceived his governing mission as that of the discerner-in-chief, an understanding rife with internal tension even if it were not flatly contradictory. Events bore Spadaro out, but there really was no way to square Francis' understanding of his mission with the expectations of his electors.[57]

Teaching and governance: Fernández in the DDF

The problems with Pope Francis' approach to curial reform and general governance of the whole Church came into sharp focus when, in July 2023, he nominated his longtime friend and sometime ghostwriter, then-Archbishop Victor Manuel Fernández, to lead the Dicastery for the Doctrine of the Faith. Historically styled *La Suprema*, owing to its elevated oversight role among the various departments of the Roman Curia, the department had seen itself sidelined during the early years of the Francis pontificate.[58] The veteran Vatican beat journalist, John L. Allen Jr., legendary for his even-handedness, even likened Francis to US President Donald Trump in each man's preference for informal "kitchen cabinet" advisors (and "keep 'em guessing" style of governance). "Close observers are well aware," Allen wrote in a 2017 analysis column[59] for *Crux*, "that when it comes to theological matters, Francis relies much more on Argentine Archbishop Victor Fernández, an old friend who heads the Pontifical Catholic University in Buenos Aires, than whoever happens to be running the CDF."

By making Fernández Prefect of the DDF (the doctrine office, formerly known as the CDF), Pope Francis rather compounded than attenuated the problem. Francis also took the highly unusual step of writing—and publishing, or causing to be published—a letter to Fernández, outlining his mission profile, the gist of which was that Francis wanted the DDF prefect to foster theological dialogue, rather than oversee doctrinal police work. "The Dicastery over which you will preside in other times came to use immoral methods," Francis wrote. "Those were times," Francis continued, "when, rather than promoting theological knowledge, possible doctrinal errors were pursued."

"What I expect from you is certainly something very different," Francis wrote. The DDF under Fernández was still "to guard the teaching that flows from the faith in order to 'to give reasons for our hope'," Francis explained, "but not as an enemy who critiques and condemns." That was an explicit reference to Francis' 2013 Apostolic Exhortation, *Evangelii gaudium*, concluding the Year of Faith proclaimed by his predecessor, Pope Benedict XVI. Fernández, it happens, had helped draft the document. Observers including this one wondered aloud at the time, what was the good of a doctrine office unbothered with doctrine?[60]

On the other hand, Pope Francis was only acknowledging in words a reality already recognized by his recent predecessors and even encouraged, albeit negatively. Pope St. John Paul II had brought the renowned German theologian, Joseph Cardinal Ratzinger, to Rome in order to head the CDF, precisely because John Paul II knew how appalling Ratzinger had found the politicisation of theology faculties in his native country. John Paul II was confident Ratzinger would be patient and restrained in the conduct of his office, as well as vigilant. Ratzinger did censure some theologians on occasion, but his censures were gentle, circumscribed, and even occasionally raised the profiles of the ones who came under them. More to the point—and a point on which there will be more to say in subsequent chapters—the idea that the doctrine office could discover and either correct or suppress every heresy in print is absurd, and always has been. It would be absurd, even if the dicastery had a hundred times the staff and extra zeroes added to its roughly €3 million annual budget.

Pope Francis rather desired Fernández, "[T]o verify that the documents," of DDF and the other dicasteries of the Roman Curia, "have an adequate theological support, are coherent with the rich humus of the perennial teaching of the Church and at the same time take into account the recent Magisterium." In an exclusive interview with *Crux* at the time of his appointment, Fernández told the digital publication, "It's not only inserting a phrase from Pope Francis, but allowing thought to be trans-figured with his criteria." Translated from the original *curialese* and put into practical terms, Francis was asking Fernández to make sure curial documents employed a sufficient number of terms from Pope Francis' rather idiosyncratic personal lexicon and otherwise reflected Francis' general outlook. A little of that is to be expected in any administration, almost as a matter of course, but the role of the doctrine dicastery historically had been to guarantee that documents of any dicastery under any pope comported well with the mind of the Church. The implicit conflation of the mind of the Church with the mind of the pope was troubling for people across the spectrum of ecclesiastical opinion, even and especially when they struggled to put their finger on what, precisely, was troubling about the new proposed arrangement.

More troubling than the unusual mission profile Pope Francis had traced for Fernández in matters of doctrine, however, was the exemption Francis carved for him with respect to the admin-istration of criminal justice, which is the DDF's other major area of competence. The DDF for many years had been responsible for investigating and prosecuting the most serious crimes at Church law, including crimes of abuse and cover-up committed against minors and vulnerable persons. In February 2022, in fact, Francis had issued *Fidem servare*—"Keeping the Faith," one of his many *motu proprio*—which formally divided the DDF into two Sections, one Doctrinal and the other Disciplinary, each with an archbishop-secretary who—on paper, at least—should report to the prefect. In essence, Francis told Fernández to leave the disciplinary part of the work to the experts.

"Given that for disciplinary matters — especially related to the abuse of minors — a specific Section has recently been created with very competent professionals," Francis wrote, "I ask you as prefect to dedicate your personal commitment more directly to the main purpose of the Dicastery, which is 'keeping the faith'." Fernández, it bears mention, came to his new job with a very chequered record on the management of abuse and cover-up cases,[61] and had even demurred when Francis first offered him the job, considering himself as he did ill-suited to the direction of DDF's disciplinary work. "[T]he Holy Father's decision for me to concentrate on doctrinal matters in no way minimizes the importance of the fight against abuse," Fernández told *Crux*. "[I]t is showing his confidence in those who know [best in these matters] so that they continue on the right path, which little by little is being consolidated."

That was a take more than a little surprising to observers across the spectrum of opinion in the Church, owing not least to the fact that DDF was at the centre of a burgeoning cover-up scandal—the Rupnik Affair—which involved several senior churchmen in the Vatican and in the worldwide Jesuit leadership, including the outgoing prefect and the chief prose-cutor at DDF—officially titled the Promoter of Justice—both Jesuits.[62] The very short version of the Rupnik Affair—an impossibly intricate and gruesome story, about which there will be much more to say in the chapter about the challenge of reform to ecclesiastical justice—is that a celebrity artist priest and erstwhile Jesuit, Marko Ivan Rupnik, had been accused by multiple highly credible witnesses, of serial spiritual, psycho-logical, and sexual abuse over decades. After years of sometimes desperate effort, victims finally found a way to make it impos-sible for the CDF/DDF to ignore the allegations. Despite copious—even mountainous—evidence, the office declined to prosecute. By midsummer 2023, the Rupnik Affair had already stained Francis' legacy.[63]

That Pope Francis should have desired a trusty friend in the top job at DDF was perhaps par for the course. The timing and manner of Fernández's appointment, however, raised serious questions. The deplorable state of justice in the Church had long since been a subject of concern. There was growing impatience among the faithful around the world, regarding the commitment of the Church's clerical and hierarchical leadership to Responsibility, Accountability, Transparency.[64] There was a crescent wariness among the worldwide secular news media, from which Francis had generally enjoyed remarkably favourable coverage. The decision to give the head office in the Vatican's top doctrinal watchdog and chief sex crimes tribunal to a fellow with Fernández's baggage, telling him not to police doctrine and also to leave the disciplinary side of the job well enough alone, was therefore rather surprising.

In form for action(?): The Church on the international stage

Every pope since St. Peter has inherited a Church in disarray. Most of the crises that became scandals during the Francis pontificate were not of Francis' making, even if his missteps in government did cause specific episodes occasioned by persistent crises to make major headlines. Experts had long since understood the crisis of abuse and cover-up in the Church to be protracted, polyvalent, pluriform, and pandemic. The financial scandals that had erupted during the Francis pontificate were likewise symptomatic of structural and cultural problems of very long standing. Francis' informal style of speaking and communicating generally made it easy for people on every side of the cultural divide to misappropriate his words for their purposes. The Church on every habitable continent, meanwhile, was facing a host of challenges peculiar and incommensurable.

In Europe, the institutional footprint of the Church was receding. The Church across Europe was plagued by the scandal—really the protracted leadership crisis—of sexual abuse and cover-up. A controversial and years-long "synodal way" in Germany had given Pope Francis great grief and dissipated the energies of the Church in Germany and throughout Europe, as well as those of the papal government and the pope himself. Francis' heavy-handed abrogation of Benedict XVI's liberalising reform allowing the use of the preconciliar 1962 order of liturgical worship caused trouble around the world and especially in France. Mass attendance continued to plummet in traditionally Catholic countries of both Eastern and Western Europe, while Francis' aforementioned missteps in handling the diplomatic crisis precipitated by the Russian invasion of Ukraine continued to cost the Church ground in public moral debate across the continent and around the world.

On that point—diplomacy—it is interesting to note that Pope Francis' greatest successes had been institutional, achieved by the work of the Holy See's experienced, dedicated, and quietly but often supremely competent professional diplomats. The diplomatic missteps of Francis' pontificate were largely the result of Francis' insistence on doing things his way and personally. Sometimes, the timing of Francis' interventions was questionable. Other times, he appeared to be working against himself. In any organization that is an international actor, the head man is ultimately responsible for policy, but the head man usually sets broad policy contours and leaves the execution to the professionals. That order in affairs was sometimes topsy turvy during the reign of Francis.

On the success side, one could think of the 2014 re-establishment, on Francis' watch, of relations between the United States and Cuba, after more than half a century of interruption. Both sides credited the breakthrough to Pope Francis personally, as well as to the diplomats who did the quiet work behind the scenes to facilitate the talks that led to the re-establishment. Francis wrote to US President Barack Obama and Raúl Castro of Cuba, urging each of the leaders to resolve "humanitarian issues" and offering to broker negotiations, which came through the good offices of Pietro Cardinal Parolin, the Secretary of State of the Holy See.

"In this case," Parolin told Vatican Radio in an exclusive interview published 18 December 2014, "the Holy See has tried to facilitate the dialogue between the two parties according to—let's say—the objective that the Holy Father, Pope Francis, has given to the diplomacy of the Holy See," an objective, "traditional in its history, but now it has [a] new emphasis—because of the situation, the particular situation of our world—which is to build bridges between persons and groups and nations." Parolin said the Holy See's diplomatic efforts were of a piece with "[w] hat we have called the culture of encounter." Parolin stressed Francis' personal role in facilitating the breakthrough, but that is just what a lieutenant does in such situations.

In Asia, the Church was experiencing significant growth as well as serious challenges. In South Korea and Japan, for example, Church numbers were growing. The Catholic Church's relations with Vietnam were warming slowly but steadily, while Pope Francis' 2024 visit to Indonesia, Papua New Guinea, East Timor, and Singapore was one of the great successes of a pontificate, the best moments of which were powerful gestures conveying the pontiff's personal touch. Francis' 2017 visit to Myanmar—after establishing diplomatic relations with the country as it struggled to establish democracy following decades of dictatorship directed by a still-entrenched military, and while there was a systematic persecution of the country's predominantly Muslim ethnic Rohingya minority ongoing—and Bangladesh, where Francis met with Rohingya refugees, was well received, also.

Francis' greatest achievement in the area of Church relations with any Asian country—and by far his most hotly debated— was his 2018 agreement with China over the appointment of bishops to Chinese sees. The agreement had been in the works for years, and was well advanced when Francis came to office in 2013. Any deal between the Holy See and mainland China was going to be controversial, but a confluence of circumstances made the one reached in 2018 radioactive for Francis. From Francis' and the Vatican's point of view, however, a bad deal with China was better than no deal. That was, paradoxically, not despite China's perceived untrustworthiness. It was precisely because the partner was untrustworthy.

For one thing, allowing civil governments some sort of say in the appointment of bishops had been the standard practice for centuries, and was standard practice in the Eastern Bloc until the collapse of the Soviet Union. For another, the Vatican's aims were not to inaugurate an Aquarian age of religious liberty in Communist China, but to prevent full-scale persecution of Chinese Catholics already struggling mightily—heroically—under the thumb (and often the boot) of a motivated, post-industrial twenty-first century totalitarian surveillance state. Francis also ardently desired to end the schism that had divided the Church in China. By those measures, the arrangement—the terms of which remain nebulous—was arguably a qualified success.

More broadly, there were other breakthroughs in the wake of the deal, like the September 2023 high-level meeting between Francis' special envoy, Matteo Cardinal Zuppi, and Chinese Minister for Eurasian Affairs, Li Hui, to discuss the ongoing Russian war of aggression in Ukraine. Not much came of the meeting between Li and Zuppi, but the fact of it—an historic first—was not nothing. None of that made the deal any better than it was—and Parolin readily admitted[65] it was highly imperfect—but China and the Vatican are both powers culturally conditioned to think in centuries. Taking the long view has its strategic advantages, but it often costs people dearly on the ground in the here-and-now.

During the Francis pontificate, both the pope and the Vatican came in for criticism—sustained and occasionally very harsh—from quarters both inside the Church and around the world, for their apparent patience with China's flagrant and documented human rights abuses. It was during the settlement period after the deal that reports of gruesome treatment of ethnic Uyghur Muslims in the west of China began to make international headlines, for example. Francis' conspicuous July 2020 decision not to condemn Chinese crackdowns on pro-Democracy demonstrators in Hong Kong was likewise the subject of powerful criticism. History has shown, time and again, how insalubrious is secular involvement in the Church's internal affairs. The Cold War-era Östpolitik of the Holy See toward

Communist powers in Europe was not exactly an unqualified success, to give only one example within living memory. At bottom, however, the problem critics saw—and continue to see—is that the Church can decide to stand for the poor and oppressed, or she can decide not to stand for the poor and oppressed, but she cannot both stand and not stand for the poor and oppressed.

Pope Leo XIV has already come face-to-face with the unwieldiness of the arrangement he inherited. During the inter-regnum, Chinese authorities announced the "election" of two bishops—one an auxiliary and the other the head of a diocese—even though there was no pope to ratify their elections. Parolin—whose term in office as Secretary of State had techni-cally ended with the decease of Pope Francis—told reporters the elections were in keeping with the agreement between the Holy See and China. The fact, however, is that such appointments are paused during papal interregna—even the ones in the works—for the very simple reason that there is no pope to make them. On 5 June 2025, Pope Leo XIV named Joseph Lin Yuntuan as auxiliary of Fuzhou diocese, and the Chinese acceded. It was evident, however, that Leo will have to work within the framework he has inherited, at least for the time being.

The Church's shifting centre of gravity

In Africa and Asia during the Francis years, the institutional footprint of the Church was growing (while longstanding problems of governance, especially an entrenched culture of abuse of girls and young women, was slowly emerging from the shadows[66]). Across the global south, leaders of the Church had long since begun to feel the shifting of the global body's centre of gravity. Pope Francis had created several new cardinals from the global south, as well. Senior churchmen, feeling their strength, were impatient with the frequently chauvinistic attitude of the Old Guard, epitomised by two incidents.

The first was an unfortunate episode involving a senior German churchman, Walter Cardinal Kasper, who told journalists covering the Ordinary General Assembly of the Synod of Bishops on the family in October 2014—the first of two highly publicized and intensely controversial Synod Assemblies on the topic—that the African bishops, "should not tell us too much what we have to do." Cool to Kasper's proposals for relaxing Church discipline regarding Communion for Catholics in irregular marital unions, and warmly opposed to Western leaders' advocacy for openness to people living "alternative" sexual lifestyles, the African bishops were not best pleased. Kasper first denied making the remark, but journalist Ed Pentin of the National Catholic Register produced a recording, so Kasper confirmed and apologised, but the damage was done.[67]

The second, more serious incident was the publication— mere days before Christmas 2023—of *Fiducia supplicans*, a document from the Dicastery of the Doctrine for the Faith asserting "the possibility of blessing couples in irregular situations and same-sex couples without officially validating their status or changing in any way the Church's perennial teaching on marriage," and attempting—in roughly five thousand words of *caveat* and qualification—to give the possibility a theological explanation. It was, charitably, Fernández's attempt to foster theological dialogue in keeping with the spirit of the mission profile Francis had traced for him. The publication of *Fiducia supplicans*, however, egregiously confused the teaching with the governing office of the Church, to spectacularly disastrous effect.

Things come to a head: *Fiducia supplicans*

Fiducia supplicans was a three-in-one calamity: a messaging failure and a communications fiasco; an ecumenical catastrophe; a debacle of governance.[68] Fernández tried to insist—in an interview with Germany's *Die Tagespost* that ran in its entirety on 3 January 2024, excerpts of which were released in *anteprima*—that the document was "a clear answer" and "a pastoral response that everyone could accept, albeit with difficulty." He tried issuing a clarification, after saying he would not be doing so. Italy's *Il Messaggero* reported[69] the Vatican's office of blessings—usually reserved for special occasions like weddings and anniversaries—inundated with requests for official parchment attestations of papal blessings for same-sex couples.[70] Activist clerics went far beyond even the latitudinous opening the document countenanced for informal private blessings, and blessed couples more or less elaborately, occasionally recording (or allowing themselves to be recorded giving) the blessings.[71]

The bishops of Africa did not buy it, and effectively revolted. So did the largest Eastern Church in full communion with Rome, the Ukrainian Greek Catholic Church (which was experiencing strained relations with Pope Francis over his lukewarm condemnation of the ongoing illegal Russia war of aggression and perceived "both-side-ism" in response to the conflict).[72] By March 2023, the Coptic Orthodox Church had suspended—temporarily, it turned out—theological dialogue[73] with the Catholic Church, citing *Fiducia supplicans* as the cause. It was a major blow to ecumenical relations, and came mere months after Francis had achieved a truly astounding ecumenical breakthrough when he recognized the canonisation of twenty-three Coptic martyrs of Libya and put them on the universal liturgical calendar of the Catholic Church.[74]

Unsustainable: Vatican finances in crisis

There is no way to sugar-coat the dire state of Vatican finances, nor any sense in trying, even if there were. The Holy See is basically insolvent. Pope Francis' early financial reform measures garnered major headlines, but his follow-through was not merely weak. It was not merely back-pedalling. It was non-existent and in fact allowed the Old Guard, impossibly antiquated in terms of skill set and general outlook when they were not corrupt, to retrench, with baleful effect. By the final weeks of his pontificate, Pope Francis had essentially given up on the financial reform. On 11 February 2025, in fact, Francis established a commission to seek donations for specific projects of the Holy See.[75]

The structural problems with the Holy See's budget have been well known to Vatican insiders since the waning days of the John Paul II pontificate, and have been before the public for well over a decade. Operating costs exceed revenues by tens of millions of dollars annually, while a burgeoning gap in the Vatican pension fund threatens to swallow the entire operation. Francis in his waning days wrote several letters to the cardinals warning of the desperate straits in which the Holy See and the Vatican City State both found themselves.

On 7 April 2025, *The Pillar* reported the Holy See showing an unfunded liability of nearly €1.5 billion in 2015—a decade before Francis established his donations commission.[76] *The Pillar*'s reporting was based on documents the investigative journalism project had obtained, and confirmed the worst. In fact, the €1.5 billion figure dwarfed earlier estimations, widely reported, which had been in the hundreds of millions of Euros. "The same documents show that Vatican financial authorities proposed measures to address the pension problem in 2015," *The Pillar* reported, adding that sources told the outfit "virtually nothing" had been done to implement the proposals in the meantime. All that put the dire warnings Francis had issued between the end of 2024 and the beginning of 2025—the last months of his pontificate—into new and garish light.

Looking forward: The papal in-tray

Pope Francis was an extraordinary man of complex character and almost preternatural force of personality, who engendered both fierce loyalty and intense opposition. His pontificate deserves the most careful and thorough treatment. Since this book is about the challenge of Catholic reform in the twenty-first century, the leadership of which effort has fallen to Pope Leo XIV, suffice it to say for now that the great frustration of the Francis pontificate—a frustration felt generally, even and especially among those well-disposed to him—was that his governance of the Church was sometimes at variance (and perhaps that it too rarely squared) with his vivid and powerfully convicting championship of ideas and causes around which Christians of every stripe and indeed all persons of good will ought to have been able to rally. Pope Leo XIV has already demonstrated not only an intuitive appreciation of the need to foster privileged spaces for genuine human conversation, but also a real knack for fostering them. That, in short, is the easy part.

This brief sketch in very broad strokes has barely touched the host of events, issues, affairs, vicissitudes fresh in the minds of churchmen and Church watchers, many of them then live issues and many still in play as Pope Leo XIV took office. It has only hinted at the interplay of forces, personalities, interests real and perceived, all of which contributed to a moment charged with tension. It has been only a panoramic view of a very difficult moment in the life of the Church, not only as she turned out of one pontificate and into another, but as she turned out of the liminal period of the early twenty-first century and into its middle. The chapters to follow will take close looks at areas urgently in need of address: Communications (and the related issues of curial culture and "synodality"), financial reform, and the administration of justice in the Church. There, the devil will be in the details.

Chapter 6

Communications, curial culture, synodality

Three major issues facing the Church will require not only address from Pope Leo XIV in fairly short order—we shall see how they have already begun to receive it—but sustained and focused attention throughout his pontificate, both looking inward and looking outward: communications, curial culture, and synodality. What these three issues have to do with one another will come into focus—one hopes—through the course of the chapter (and those to follow). For now, suffice it to say that repairing the broken communications culture in the Vatican is mission-critical because the Church's whole purpose is to communicate the Good News of salvation to the whole world, while the Roman Curia serves the pope in his mission of teaching, sanctifying, and governing the Church in the world, and synodality is the name of the great—albeit inchoate—insight of the Francis pontificate, full of potential and therefore of danger, not entirely unlike an open construction site.

Robert Francis Prevost OSA was in Rome for significant stretches over the last quarter-century, from 2001–13 as prior general of the Order of Saint Augustine, and again in 2023, when Pope Francis named him to serve as prefect of the Dicastery for Bishops. Prevost observed, closely but from a position of institutional remove, the strengths and weaknesses not only of Roman curial government but of Vatican communications culture specifically. He also felt the power of Vatican communications in his life as a missionary priest and bishop.

That is only one reason why Leo XIV's 19 June 2025 visit to the Vatican's shortwave transmission facility was so significant.

The visit to the broadcast centre in Santa Maria di Galeria, located some 17km outside the Rome city limits (to the northwest, almost exactly halfway between the Ottavia neighbourhood on the very outskirts of the city and Lake Bracciano), got little attention in the press. The mere fact of it was powerfully telling. If Leo had desired merely to offer a general word of encouragement to Vatican communications staff, he could have saved himself the trouble and gone down the *Via della Conciliazione* a few hundred yards to the prefect's office, or a little further to the main production centre in Palazzo Pio, which faces Castel Sant'Angelo. Leo could have visited either or both, without even crossing the river. Instead, he went to the shortwave station outside town. That he visited the shortwave centre on the 43rd anniversary of his own priestly ordination only adds to the sense of pitch and moment in the visit.

The shortwave transmission centre opened in 1957, with a broadcast room designed by renowned engineer and architect Pier Luigi Nervi (designer also of the Paul VI audience hall, popularly known in Rome as the *Sala Nervi*). The sprawling facility—an extra-territorial holding of the Holy See, meaning it is not subject to Italian state jurisdiction—covers more than a thousand acres and boasts some two dozen antennae emitting both short-wave and medium-wave (AM) signals. In the 1990s and into the 2010s, the facility was the subject of protracted litigation over its alleged output of electromagnetic energy in excess of Italian legal limits. In 2012—several years before the wider reform project began under Pope Francis—the Vatican announced plans to begin curtailing broadcast hours from the site and eventually to halve them, while the major reform under Francis considered but never executed plans to phase out shortwave entirely. The last pope to visit the site was John Paul II in 1991.

A 19 June 2025 statement from the press office noted how Pope Leo XIV, during his visit to the Santa Maria di Galeria facility, remarked the crucial role shortwave transmissions from Vatican Radio played in his own ministry and—more importantly—in the lives of the people to whom he ministered. People within Vatican Radio knew and understood the power of the medium, especially shortwave. Difficult to regulate and virtually impossible to block, shortwave is a powerful tool for reaching people in places not only geographically remote but politically isolated. If the people in charge of implementing the reforms desired by Pope Francis had understood the power of the medium, however, they gave little sign of it during their conduct of reform efforts.

"Pope Leo emphasized how during his missionary work in Latin America and Africa, it was valuable to be able to receive Vatican Radio's shortwave transmissions, which reach places where few broadcasters can reach, and he reaffirmed the missionary value of communication," the statement from the press office described Leo as telling his staff at the Santa Maria di Galeria site. Leo's years of service as a missionary priest and later bishop in Peru were stretched over more than 30 years, from the 1980s into the 2020s, while his experience of Africa was largely through visits to various places on the continent—especially Kenya, where the Order of Saint Augustine has a significant presence—and relatively recent. His note of shortwave's perduring importance in the lives of people in both Latin America and especially Africa is therefore itself noteworthy, inasmuch as it complicates—to say the least—a prevailing point in the preferred narrative of the erstwhile reform architects, in essence that terrestrial radio had already become obsolete even in the still developing and impoverished regions of the global south.

Leo also visited a property on the Santa Maria di Galeria site where a project for an agrisolar (dual-use agricultural and photovoltaic) plant is under study, with the eventual purpose of providing for the energy needs of the Vatican City State. Pope Francis approved the project in a 21 June 2024 *motu proprio, Fratello sole*—"Brother Sun"—giving responsibility to the president of the Vatican City government and the head of the Holy See's sovereign asset manager. It is noteworthy, perhaps, that the language of Francis' order assumed the radio station would continue to broadcast. "I entrust to you," Francis wrote, "the task of constructing an agrivoltaic plant located within the extraterritorial zone of Santa Maria di Galeria that will guarantee, not only the power supply of the radio station there, but also the complete energy sustenance of Vatican City State."

Exactly how Leo will use the means of communication available to him, is something that remains largely to be seen. It is certain that Leo appreciates the power of various media. It is evident that he knows how to convey messages across them and through them and with them. He understands that the management of precious resources under conditions of scarcity in a world with limitless demands, endlessly shifting in their intensity and urgency, requires both ruthless mission discipline and a human touch.

The challenge of reform: Vatican Communications

The perfect nexus of the reform challenge facing Pope Leo XIV in these regards is to be found in the practical case of the Vatican communications apparatus. The Dicastery for Communication of the Holy See is the umbrella organ under which—on paper at least—the various offices and department and outfits of the communications apparatus are now organized. The Holy See used to have a semi-official state broadcaster, Vatican Radio, a daily newspaper, a publishing house, a translation service, and several other minor offices, as well as a press office. As of 2016, however, those formerly independent outfits—independent of each other, for sure, and Vatican Radio was a juridically independent and free-standing organization with its own autonomous leadership structure, by-laws, assets, and staff—began to be brought under the aegis of what was originally styled the Secretariat for Communication.

The name was important. Like the Secretariat of State and the Secretariat for the Economy (the latter created in 2014), the Secretariat for Communication was to be a point of reference for the entire curial system, with powers to coordinate work across departments. Pope Francis ordered the name changed to Dicastery for Communication in June of 2018, after a major fake news scandal involving the Secretariat's inaugural prefect. The 2022 Apostolic Constitution overhauling the whole curial structure made it clear that the new communications organization would not be exercising anything like the coordinating role originally suggested.

Whether one considers the general curial reform begun under Pope Francis to be a work in progress requiring completion, or an ill-conceived effort best scratched and begun afresh, or a sound plan imperfectly undertaken and poorly executed, is largely beside the point. Vatican communications are a shambles, and have been for a very long time. This is despite great expense of money and other resources, despite a highly competent core of professionals across the various communications departments and organs within the Vatican system, despite those professionals being primed and ready for reform and among the most highly motivated Vatican employees, almost universally well-disposed to the institutions supposed to support and execute their part of the Holy See's mission. The Vatican's communications culture is broken, in short, but the lion's share of blame for that is not to be lodged with the workaday professionals in the communications organs.

As Charles Collins put it in a piece titled "Why it may take 'a little violence' to fix Vatican communications," a powerfully insightful analysis published by *Crux* on 5 May 2017, "That major work needs doing is perhaps the one thing on which everyone agrees." Collins, who spent 15 years at Vatican Radio, 2002–17, wrote that he "[did] not recall ever hearing anyone – no layperson, at least – contest the idea that a major reform of Vatican communications is past due." I worked with Collins in that system, on the English-language news desk at

Vatican Radio, from 2005–17. During those dozen years from the summer of 2005 until 31 December 2017, the power and limitations not only of the communications apparatus but also—in some ways primarily—the communications culture in the Vatican generally came into sharp focus. The reform began in earnest under Pope Francis in 2016, on the back of two major external consultations. There was resistance to the reforms, not because people in the departments did not see the need for reform, but because of the shape and driving ethos of the reform effort.[77]

"Over the years," noted the legendary Vatican beat journalist and editor-in-chief of *Crux*, John L. Allen Jr., in presenting the aforementioned analysis piece by Collins for a 2017 retrospective round-up of the year that had been, "most of the real communications breakdowns in the Vatican haven't come from the offices [then] being overhauled, but from cardinals and other bigwigs who put their foot in their mouth at the just-wrong moment." Allen also noted—again following Collins—how the erstwhile head of the then-recently consolidated communications apparatus, Msgr. Dario Edoardo Viganò (no relation to the celebrity whistleblower-turned-crackpot conspiracy theorist and excommunicate, Archbishop Carlo Maria Viganò), would have difficulty in such a lofty billet. A cleric of such low rank (a monsignor is not even a bishop, let alone an archbishop or a cardinal) was always going to face difficulty bringing the very much senior prelates of other dicasteries to heel.[78]

Viganò, it happened, would resign under a cloud in 2018 after he misrepresented the answer Pope emeritus Benedict XVI gave to a request—rebuffed by the former pope—for a contribution to a collection of essays on the theology of Pope Francis, then doctored a photographic image of Benedict's letter spelling out the reasons for his refusal of the request.[79] It was a fake news scandal, in essence, and a terrible embarrassment for Francis on the heels of his Message for World Day for Social Communications dedicated to the evil of fake news.[80] Pope Francis eventually replaced Viganò with a layman, Dr.

Paolo Ruffini, who would distinguish himself principally for his stalwart defence of his department's use of artwork by an accused serial rapist (about which there is much more to say in chapters to come).

The problems facing Vatican communications, in short, were not primarily with the rank and file of the various communications outfits, nor even—with some notable exception—the chiefs of the various offices, of which there were nearly a dozen: the Press Office of the Holy See, Vatican Radio, the *Centro Televisivo Vaticano*, *L'Osservatore Romano*, the *Libreria Editrice Vaticana* (the publishing house), the Vatican Information Service (under the aegis of the Press Office), *inter alia*. The problems were structural and cultural. There were several outfits reporting on the same papal and Vatican events and stories, often with little in the way of even informal communication internally.

Most importantly, however, there was no overarching office to train, staff, and direct the communications efforts of the various departments and offices within the Roman Curia, a problem at once cultural and structural. The senior leaders and top staffers in the various Vatican departments operate in silos. That is problematic in and of itself—a problem of curial culture—indirectly related to the problem of communications culture, namely that only a few curial departments even have their own communications desks. The communications officers who staff those desks are not "in the room" as a matter of course. Nor, for that matter, is the director of the press office of the Holy See in the room for papal meetings with senior curial leadership or other decision-makers. For the pope and for departments with public-facing profiles, this cultural fact leads with some frequency to embarrassment and worse.

The pope, in short, has neither a communications director nor a communications directorate to speak of. Communications people do not help craft messaging. They are informed of policy and given directives after decisions are taken. In the main, senior clerical and hierarchical leaders do not seek their opinion when crafting policy or making decisions, nor do they usually invite the communications people to participate in policy discussions. For the better part of a hundred years, the opposite has been true in most government departments around the world. There are times when leaders and policymakers need to ask the communications people to step out of the room, but that is because the comms people are in the room.

Pope Leo XIV can fix that. He can order the creation of a permanent communications liaison in every department of the Roman Curia, and order that the department heads or their deputies meet at least weekly to share information. He can appoint people to senior leadership who know what communications officers are supposed to do and how they are supposed to serve the mission. Most importantly, he can lead by example in these regards.

In terms of the existing apparatus, Pope Leo XIV will have to find a way to make economies. He will need to galvanize a demoralized workforce. He will need to identify leaders who think with the mind of the Church, understand the message focus of the reigning pontiff, see what a vast and irreplaceable treasure they have in the rank and file of workaday professionals staffing the communications apparatus, and are adept not only at the use of new technologies but comprehend their logic. Leo will need to put such leaders in place, find them the resources they need, and then get out of their way.

The principal challenge for Pope Leo XIV in these regards presents itself with facets facing at once *ad intra* and *ad extra*. The reform of Vatican communications, for example, is not merely a matter of good public relations or even best practice in government—though it is both of those things—but is crucial to the Church's core mission, which is to spread the Gospel, the εὐαγγέλιον, the Good News of salvation. People across the spectrum of opinion in the Church will inevitably agree with some of any pope's decisions and disagree with others, and they will occasionally speak frankly both in agreement and disagreement, so it is vitally important that everyone have the best possible information regarding matters in the public interest, as quickly and directly as possible. If people cannot trust the pope's own communications apparatus to give it to them straight—at least, not to give it to them crooked—then they will have a hard time trusting not only the pope but any churchman and indeed any Christian.

Communication as listening: "Synodality" and the Synod of Bishops

The "other" half of communication is listening. "[W]hat specifically makes communication good and fully human," Pope Francis wrote in his 24 January 2022 Message for World Communications Day, "is listening to the person in front of us, face to face, listening to the other person whom we approach with fair, confident, and honest openness." Francis spoke often, in fact, of his desire to foster a culture of listening in the Church. Francis was vocal and insistent throughout his pontificate in his calls for a more "synodal" Church, a key to which—he said—is listening.

"Synodality" was a keyword of Francis' pontificate, albeit one with little in the way of real articulation, despite copious expense of verbiage on the subject from Francis' appointed lieutenants tasked with the management of "synodal" business. Francis used an existing institution, the Synod of Bishops, to promote synodality. There were a series of Synod Assemblies over several years, roughly the last third of the Francis pontificate, dedicated to synodality. There were meetings at the parish, diocesan, regional, national, and continental levels between the major gatherings in Rome. A great deal of time, energy, and money—no one has been able to say how much of that last—went into the promotion of synodality, but never produced a straightforward working definition of synodality beyond the idea that it is a broadly consultative style of government.

The lack of concrete sense or even clear contour created the impression that synodality was in effect a buzzword, largely devoid of content and destined to pass into oblivion with a few years, at most. There were sizeable contingents across the spectrum of opinion in the Church who looked to that day with a measure of relief. There were plenty of reasons acting as drivers of that sentiment. The Synod of Bishops as such, however, is an organ with enormous potential, largely untapped.

The institution known as the Synod of Bishops, created in 1965 by Pope St. Paul VI in the wake of the Vatican Council II as a consultative body, often functioned as a talking shop for popes. Pope Francis used the institution in that way, but he also went further. Francis' 2018 reform of the Synod of Bishops became an emblem of his more autocratic tendencies. Francis gave the body permanence as a Church structure answerable to the pope, erected outside the Roman curial structure. Basically, he made the body a permanent pontifical rubber stamp.

When Pope Francis permanently erected the Secretariat of the Synod of Bishops outside the Roman Curia in 2018, he altered some mechanics of the body, but he gave it no real governing power. At least, he gave the Synod of Bishops no power the body could exercise without the pope. Francis also arranged matters so, that the pope could make the Synod say whatever the pope wished the Synod to say. There was nothing wrong with any of that, but he also greatly empowered the General Secretariat of the Synod of Bishops to manage not only General Assemblies but also activities of the Synod between assemblies.

Pope Leo XIV gave fairly short shrift to the General Secretariat of the Synod of Bishops when he met with them for the first time on 26 June 2025. "I cannot remain with you all afternoon," Leo told them. "I would be happy to take this opportunity to share an idea that I consider central," he continued, "and then to listen to you in the time available to me." The idea he shared was, in essence, that the Synod of Bishops is what its origi-nator, Pope St. Paul VI, created it to be. "The Synod of Bishops naturally retains its institutional physiognomy," Leo told the Secretariat, "and at the same time is enriched by the fruits that have matured in this season," of reflection under Pope Francis, who made "synodality" a major focus of the Secretariat's and the Church's official energies. "During his pontificate," Leo said, "Pope Francis carried forward this concept in the various Synodal Assemblies, especially in those on the family, and then made it flow into the latest path, dedicated precisely to synodality."

"[T]he legacy [Pope Francis] has left us," Leo continued, "seems to me to be above all this: that synodality is a style, an attitude that helps us to be Church, promoting authentic experiences of participation and communion." Whatever that means, it is not the stuff of radical revolution in the Church's self-understanding, nor is it the stuff on which an engine of radical institutional change will ever run. Proponents of "synodality" had struggled for nearly a dozen years to say what it was. Francis himself admitted the notion was nebulous even in his own mind, even as he worked to give the idea power and to make it a force shaping the Church's modes and orders of government. In a few short sentences, Leo reduced the legacy of Francis's efforts to a "style" with at most an ancillary role to play in the Church's life.

The Secretariat of the Synod of Bishops had come to have a high profile under Leo's predecessor and had been insulated— to some extent, at least—against Pope Francis' fairly regular and rather abrasive remonstrations with curial officials. Pope Leo did not assail the Secretariat the way Francis had inveighed against curial departments and their officials. It was not necessary. He gently, but unmistakably, put them in their place and on notice. It was a master class in *Romanitas*, the distinctive Roman way of doing things.

Romanitas

Many of the rank-and-file workers in offices and departments within the Vatican felt consistently hard pressed and occasionally hard done by Pope Francis, who sharply criticized them and frequently governed without them. Pope Leo XIV, by contrast, was most careful to express gratitude for the work of curial officials high and low, and solicitude for their well-being. When Leo received the employees of the Holy See and the Vatican City State on Saturday, 24 May 2025, "Thank you," were almost the first words he spoke. "This first meeting of ours is certainly not the moment to make keynote speeches," Leo said, "but rather it is an opportunity for me to thank you for the service you carry out, and this service that I have, so to speak, 'inherited' from my predecessors."

If Leo has inherited the Roman Curia, it is also the case that the Roman Curia has come into Leo, as well. Leo went on to quote a maxim of *Romanitas*: "Popes come and go," he said, "the Curia remains." Leo stressed the crucial institutional role of the Curia and of curial officials, noting how the Curia "is the institution that preserves and transmits the historical memory of a Church, of the ministry of its bishops," an important role. "[T]o work in the Roman Curia means to contribute to keeping the memory of the Apostolic See alive," said Leo, "so that the Pope's ministry may be implemented in the best way."

"[B]y analogy," Leo immediately added, "this can also be said of the services of Vatican City State." While one may accuse this old Vatican hand of too much subtlety in reading for what follows, it nevertheless bears mention that Leo operates in that remark a crucial distinction: between the Holy See and the Vatican City State. Leo noted that his remarks regarding the Roman Curia may be said, by analogy, also of the services of the Vatican City State. Leo was not speaking loosely. "By analogy," in the mouth of Leo, does not indicate mere similarity in some respects. The relation of the Vatican City State to the Holy See, he was saying, is like the relation of a creature to its creator.

The Holy See is the sovereign subject of international law that is the juridical expression of the Apostolic See—the pope—in the world. The Roman Curia is the governing and administrative apparatus of the Holy See, hence the central governing and administrative apparatus of the Catholic Church worldwide. The Vatican City State is the sovereign territory of the Holy See, with its own organs and structures of government, its own infrastructure—police force, fire department, healthcare system, maintenance staff, etc.—and its own general institutional footprint. Most of what most people mean when they say "the Vatican"—really little more than an imprecise journalistic shorthand—belongs not to the Vatican City State, but to the Holy See.

A complete rehearsal of the ways in which Pope Francis' piecemeal and *ad hoc* legislation muddied the distinction, is far beyond the scope of this book. Suffice it to say, with veteran Vatican analyst Andrea Gagliarducci (who coined the term and carefully chronicled it through all the years of the Francis pontificate), that there was under Francis a "Vaticanisation of the Holy See" with consequences that were never entirely unproblematic and occasionally far-reaching at least in their potential repercussions. In framing the issue as he did, Pope Leo XIV once again showed himself to be a master of rhetoric. Leo at once reassured his closest collaborators and gave them a morale boost, while also gently but unequivocally acknowledging a major institutional confusion that had been getting worse for several years under his predecessor.

There were three other particularly noteworthy points in Pope Leo XIV's remarks to curial officials, discrete but intricately related to one another, which merit some close consideration. One is Leo's sensibility of the Roman Curia's institutional role not only in the Vatican but for the papacy and the Church, which speaks to Leo's character as an institutionalist. Another is his specific appreciation for the Curia's—hence for curial officers'—duty to preserve the institutional memory of the papacy, for all the men who come in turns to the papal office and for the whole worldwide body of Christians through generations in history, which further attests the profoundly Augustinian cast of Leo's mind. The last is rather biographical—

or autobiographical—and concerns Leo's experience over several decades of his life as a missionary priest and bishop.

Institutional memory

When Pope Leo XIV said, "The Curia is the institution that preserves and transmits the historical memory of a Church, of the ministry of its bishops," he meant not only the Roman Curia, but those of "every particular Church, for the episcopal Curiae," as well. He was saying something of crucial importance regarding how he understands the institution of the Church in its every articulation. Curiae are bureaucracies, to be sure, but they are also the *cor*—the heart, in the Augustinian sense—of the People of God on pilgrimage through history, in hierarchical communion, on their way to eternity.

For the Augustinian, memory is not merely a storehouse of the past but the threefold presence of all time: a power of the mind to make present the past, yes, but also the presence of the present and the presence of the future. Saint Augustine of Hippo devoted the entirety of Book X of his *Confessions* to a magnificent exploration of memory, which is among the very greatest philosophical and literary achievements of all time. Memory, to the Augustinian, is not only nor even primarily a power of mere factual and procedural recall—though it is also that—but the power that keeps our origin in God before us, His constant work in and through and around and about us all throughout our lives, and our destiny with Him.

Memory, in a word, is the seat of the self. "Memory," Leo said, "is an essential element in a living organism. It is not only directed to the past, but nourishes the present and guides the future. Without memory, the path is lost, it loses its sense of direction." When Leo charged the Roman Curia with the preservation and transmission of the historical memory of the See of Peter, he was saying something monumentally significant. By indicating at once the peculiarity of the Roman Curia and the universality of the curial mission in its articulate presence in all the Churches, he was acknowledging not only the fact, but the mode of communion-in-memory and communion-as-memory that unites the whole Church through all time and into eternity. The Church is at once a very human institution and a divinely constituted mystical body.

More prosaically, the Roman Curia is in fact a very large and very old chancery, which has existed in some form ever since St. Peter—the first bishop of Rome—looked over one of his shoulders and asked someone to take a letter. It ought to be a model for other curial outfits, not in its peculiar *modus operandi*, but in the single-mindedness of its focus on the work, which is the work of government. The Roman Curia, in short, is a bureaucracy: a power structure. Pope Francis' Apostolic Constitution, *Praedicate Evangelium*, was—in part, at least—an attempt to give the Roman Curia a permanent missionary élan. That may sound pretty when one first hears it, but it does not withstand scrutiny.

"The main point of the new Apostolic Constitution, *Praedicate Evangelium*, is that the mission of the Church is evangelisation," Oswald Cardinal Gracias—a member of Pope Francis' "kitchen cabinet" Council of Cardinal Advisors and an architect of the curial reform law—told Spanish-language *Vida Nueva* magazine in 2019. "[*Praedicate Evangelium*] puts evangelisation at the centre of the Church, and of everything the Curia does," Gracias also said in the interview. "[The Dicastery for] Evangelisation," he explained, would therefore be the "first dicastery" in the new system. In reality—more complex and profoundly human than any drafting effort—the reform of the Curia merely reconfigured for a moment the power struggles between and among the various departments, which saw the last vestiges of internal mission-focus swept away by *Praedicate Evangelium*. The idea of making evangelisation the mission of the Curia sounded like a worthy purpose—it might even have been a lofty cause—but it did not account for what the Curia is, let alone for how it does its work.

To the extent that making evangelisation the central focus of the Roman Curia's work really was the lodestar of Francis' reform, the effort did two things: it "put ideas above reality," which ran squarely counter to one of Pope Francis' own favourite maxims of conduct; it sought to force the Roman Curia to be something it could not ever be, or at least to do something it was not designed to do. The Roman Curia, in short, is a power structure: a bureaucracy. Making evangelisation its mission did not—nor could it ever—make the Roman Curia fit for ecclesial purpose. Such an effort could only ever succeed in bureaucratizing the Church's missionary mandate.

The Roman Curia exists to assist the pope in governing the Church. The papal office is a missionary office because it is the supreme teaching, sanctifying and governing office of the Church, which is an essentially missionary society. Pope Francis—who also spoke often and eloquently of memory—was absolute in his insistence on the urgency of the need for the Church to recover the sense of herself as missionary. Pope Leo XIV recognizes the same reality, but puts it in an institutional framework. "[T]he experience of mission forms part of my life, and not only as a baptized person, as for all us Christians, but because as an Augustinian religious I was a missionary in Peru, and in the midst of the Peruvian people my pastoral vocation matured," Leo said in his speech to curial and Vatican City staffers. "Then," Leo said, "the call [came] to serve the Church here in the Roman Curia was a new mission, which I shared with you during these last two years," in the leadership of the Dicastery for Bishops, "and still I continue it and will continue it, as long as God wills, in this service that has been entrusted to me."[81]

In short

As Fr. Robert Francis Prevost OSA, and later as Bishop Robert Francis Prevost OSA of Chiclayo, Peru, and then as Robert

Francis Cardinal Prevost OSA, Prefect of the Dicastery for Bishops, the man we know now as Pope Leo XIV has been in turns subject to diocesan curial government (though as a religious priest, never directly or wholly) and in charge of a diocesan curia (that of Chiclayo), subject to the Roman Curia and then head of a powerful Roman department. He understands, from long and various experience, the power of curial outfits for good and for ill, to help and to hinder both clerics and the faithful in their missionary efforts. It bears mention in these regards, that his 12 years in the worldwide leadership of his Order of Saint Augustine as prior general also gave him experience of the peculiar ways in which the Roman Curia can help and hinder religious life in the Church.

It would be reasonable, after all that, to wonder what the fuss has been about. After all, what is doing in Rome has little bearing on the day-to-day of Christians' lives in the world, not even on the lives of Christians who happen to live in Rome. On the other hand, the knock-on effects of dysfunction in government are felt broadly and deeply. Said bluntly, Catholics can debate the relative merits of this or that doctrinal question, whether this papal pronouncement is good or bad, whether the pope ought to have done the thing or ought not to have done, but someone must keep the lights on and wheels turning.

Chapter 7

Financial reform

Pope Leo XIV, by accepting his election, may well have done the one thing that will keep the lights on and the wheels turning in the Vatican, at least for a little while. The Vatican has been facing a massive and growing budget crisis, and has spent far more than it has brought in for several years running. There is a gaping hole in the operating budget of the Holy See, in short, while an unfunded pension liability has been screaming for urgent structural address since no later than 2015 (and really since the years before Pope Francis was elected in 2013). It need not have been any part of the cardinals' calculations when they were in conclave or when they were preparing for conclave, but if they were not thinking of the bump in donations the election of *un americano* to Peter's See was likely to occasion, they ought to have been. In any case, even a very significant uptick in donations from one country—or from several countries— would be no more than a stopgap.

Misconceptions

There is an idea, widely held, according to which "the Vatican" sits like Smaug atop a vast hoard of material wealth. It is easy to understand how one comes to the idea. The Vatican Museums are among the largest in the world—fifth, in terms of floor space—and second in the world in terms of visitors, owing to the Museums' genuinely stupefying collection. The Holy See has a sizeable real estate portfolio, as well, a fact that also lends itself to misconception. The Museums generate ticket sales, which help to fund the operations of the Vatican City State. The real estate portfolio, while it could certainly be managed much better than it is at present, in fact contains many assets that would be considered toxic if they were commercial concerns.

The Holy See rents properties to religious orders and congregations at very friendly rates, for example, allowing them to have a central bureaucratic and administrative presence in Rome and to conduct good works—shelters, kitchens, laundries, various other forms of apostolic outreach—throughout Italy, primarily. The Holy See essentially subsidizes the works of these religious orders and congregations. The art in the Museums' collections, on the other hand, is literally priceless—part of the common patrimony of humanity—and could not be bought or sold in any case. The same goes for the Vatican-owned basilicas and other church buildings, which do not bring in rent or other revenue and in fact are quite costly to keep.

Adding to the misconceptions concerning Vatican finances is a misapprehension of the Catholic Church's articulate structure. Dioceses and archdioceses are not branches of the Vatican. They are juridical persons in their own right, with their own assets (and liabilities), personnel, subsidiary institutions and organs of government. Dioceses that are able to do so, make contributions to the Holy See. Those contributions, however, do not come close to covering costs of operation.

The total operating budget for the Holy See in 2022—the last year for which there are complete figures published—was €769.6 million, or $905 million (at the current exchange rate). In that same year, 2022, the Holy See estimated total financial assets at €1.8 billion. The 2024 balance sheet of the Administration of the Patrimony of the Apostolic See—APSA, the Holy See's sovereign wealth manager—put the value of APSA's total patrimony at just shy of €2.6 billion and reported a diminution of €145 million since 2023. APSA released its 2024 report on 28 July 2025, making it the first major financial report—though not a complete effective budget—of the new Leonine era. The report also indicated continued real estate sell-offs, with the total number of properties owned by the Holy See down from 4,249 in 2023 to 4,234 in 2024.

It would be easy to get lost in the weeds of the report—indeed, it is tempting—but the big takeaways are in the total numbers. To give an idea of how small the financial footprint of the Holy See really is, consider that the 2025 operating budget of the largest Catholic university in the United States, Notre Dame University in South Bend, Indiana, was $1.89 billion (roughly €1.62 billion in 2025). That is twice the Holy See's operating budget for 2022, and the Holy See is the central governing apparatus for a global organization with 1.4 billion members. Notre Dame's endowment, meanwhile, dwarfs the Holy See's total reported holdings in both 2022 and 2024, with the university reporting an endowment of $20.1 billion.[82]

If it is only fair to note that the Holy See does a very great deal with what is really very little, it is also the case that the Holy See could—should—do much better. There are cultural, structural, historical, political, and other contingent reasons the Holy See does not do anywhere near as well as it is reasonable to expect. The money scandals that have plagued the Vatican in recent years and decades, however, were very much the result of a toxic combination of short-sightedness, arrogance, incompetence, and workaday corruption. All that is part of the story, too.

Peter's Pence: Myth, facts, conjecture

Since the years following the collapse of the papal states in 1870, a main source of income for the Holy See has been the annual worldwide Peter's Pence collection (known in Italian as the *Obolo di San Pietro*). For decades, the Holy See has used the proceeds of Peter's Pence to plug the gaping holes in the operating budget. There is nothing wrong with that. The

Vatican, however, advertised the collection as an opportunity for the faithful to participate in the pope's charitable activities on behalf of the world's very neediest, and couched the lines describing the use of Peter's Pence to keep the bureaucracy running very carefully, indeed. When that fact began to be widely known—and it did, beginning in the early part of the 2010s—the faithful were not best pleased.

The feeling was that the Vatican was soliciting donations on false pretences, and the feeling was not wrong. Bishops around the world—who knew better than the faithful where the money was going, or should have known—did not go out of their way to supply the faithful with more complete disclosure of the monies' destinations. In January 2020, the Dallas, TX-based Stanley Law Group filed a class action lawsuit in the United States District Court for the District of Rhode Island against the United States Conference of Catholic Bishops (USCCB), claiming the US bishops' conference fraudulently promoted Peter's Pence.[83] The lawsuit stalled in 2022, but the message was sent and the damage done. Donations, which had been falling off for some time, plummeted.

A convergence of causes contributed to the collapse in giving. A story in December 2019 by Francis X. Rocca of the *Wall Street Journal* reported that no more than ten per cent of donations actually went to the poor and needy in any given year. That story made the rounds and even figured in the class action filing in the US in January 2020. Donations from around the world fell off, driven down by other related factors as well, including the relentlessly atrocious news cycle that began in 2018 and continued through 2019 (which included the Barros Affair in Chile, the McCarrick scandal and others in the United States, *inter alia*[84]), and by the economic disruption of the Covid-19 pandemic that essentially halted worldwide tourism and put a major dent in Vatican Museums' ticket sales, another major source of revenue for the Vatican City State.[85]

Over the years, the Holy See had invested some of the annual Peter's Pence collection in a Peter's Pence Fund. The capital had grown significantly. Between 2015 and 2020, however, the Holy See spent more from Peter's Pence than the annual collection brought in. "The *Obolo* fund has been decapitalized in recent years due to the expenses of the Curia's dicasteries, which needed more than what was being collected," then-Prefect of the Secretariat for the Economy, Fr. Juan Antonio Guerrero Alves SJ, told the official Vatican News service in 2021.[86] Guerrero reported that the total value of the Peter's Pence fund fell from €319 million to €205 million. "It is obvious that this can no longer continue," Guerrero said, not wrongly.

Through the last years of the Francis pontificate, however, spending from Peter's Pence continued to outstrip revenue significantly. The one year in which income did outstrip spending was 2022, but the income reported was from a massive sell-off: €107 million in income against €93 million in spending. Nearly €64 million of the €107 million total came from the sale of assets. In 2023, spending was nearly double income. In 2024, spending outstripped income by roughly 30 per cent.[87]

One of the very significant "groundwork" changes that took place during the Francis pontificate was the improvement of transparency regarding Peter's Pence. The Peter's Pence website, in fact, has made its reports of income and spending not only available but more readily accessible online. The Holy See, however, does not disclose information regarding total cash reserves, making it difficult to estimate how long the Holy See can continue with deficit spending. If the massive sell-off in 2022 is any indication, it cannot be long.

Signs of the times

There are other indications of impending disaster, as well. In 2020, Pope Francis began to implement a planned consolidation of all Holy See assets under the management of the Administration of the Patrimony of the Apostolic See—APSA, the Holy See's sovereign wealth manager—partly in response to scandals involving the Secretariat of State (which had its own discretionary and other stable funds) like the highly publicized Sloane Ave. real estate debacle that has been an ongoing embarrassment for the Holy See. The Sloane Ave. scandal involved a poorly conceived and ineptly managed €250 million investment of the Holy See's Secretariat of State in a real estate development project located at the old Harrods warehouse in the Chelsea neighbourhood of London. The very short version of an implausibly long and impossibly convoluted story is that the Vatican found a way to lose money—lots of it—on a blue-chip London real estate investment, and saw Pope Francis change the law several times to facilitate the trial of Giovanni Angelo Cardinal Becciu and eight other defendants in Vatican City criminal court on charges of financial and other official malfeasance in connection with the deal. The whole saga features not only a real estate investment gone bad, but supporting characters taken from central casting: shady businessmen, a femme fatale, feuding attorneys on both sides, a judge with ties to Italy's most infamous missing persons case (also involving the Vatican), and—of course—a cardinal at the centre of the whole business, who swears he is innocent. Becciu is appealing his conviction on various financial crimes.

If those scandals were the occasion for the reforms, they were not the sole and perhaps not the primary reason for them. The expansion of APSA's direct responsibility for the management not only of real but also moveable and liquid curial assets once held discretely by the various dicasteries was solidified in legislation following Pope Francis' Apostolic Constitution reforming the entire Roman Curia, *Praedicate Evangelium*. In August 2022, Pope Francis issued a rescript "clarifying" that exclusive competence for managing all of the Holy See's movable and liquid assets rests with the Institute for the Works of Religion—the IOR, commonly though inaccurately called the "Vatican Bank"—and ordering the various dicasteries and other entities of the Holy See to transfer all financial assets to the IOR, poste-haste.[88] *Praedicate* had disposed that dicasteries should conduct transactions through the IOR. The rescript gave IOR the management of those assets, meaning that the various dicasteries and other entities of the Holy See needed to deposit their liquid assets with the IOR—which, as Ed Condon of *The Pillar* noted at the time[89]—potentially subjected the assets and the dicasteries to international oversight (not necessarily a bad thing).

The 2022 move by Pope Francis may have been a rare and much belated win for the inaugural Prefect of the Secretariat for the Economy, George Cardinal Pell, who had advocated for a similar move from the outset of his reform mission. Pope Francis, in fact, had created the Secretariat for the Economy in 2014 and given the department and its prefect sweeping powers to investigate, compel, and otherwise act to put the Holy See in financial order. In 2015, Francis also appointed the Vatican's first-ever auditor-general, Libero Milone, only to let him be forced into resigning a year later after police interrogation and fairly frog-marched to the Vatican City gate. The cardinal who obtained the resignation was none other than Giovanni Angelo Becciu, later convicted of criminal financial malfeasance in the aforementioned Sloane Ave. affair. Pell died in 2023, but Milone lives as of this writing, and continues to fight what he considers—with many observers—to have been his unjust dismissal, and claims he holds the receipts to show that the real reason he was unceremoniously removed was his discovery of corruption and incompetence staggering in scope and scale.

The 2024 APSA report, in any case, had a line for APSA's moveable assets, as well, raising the question whether—and if so, to what extent—there has been effective compliance with the 2022 order. Understanding what the law is at present, will itself be a major headache for Pope Leo XIV. There had been so many changes atop so many others during the Francis pontificate, that it was difficult even for experts to understand what the state of affairs really was. Getting to the bottom of the business before the money runs out is now Leo's responsibility.

A threefold challenge for Pope Leo XIV

Pope Leo XIV needs to increase donations to Peter's Pence significantly and sustainably. In order to do that, he will need to be both rigorously honest and completely forthright with the worldwide body of the faithful, especially regarding where and how he spends the money. That is more easily said than done, especially in the current climate. Leo will also need to make economies—real economies—in the meantime, which are not on the backs of overworked and undercompensated staffers, many of whom have not had a raise in years, even as their workloads have increased and their overtime compensation in coin has been reduced. Leo will also need to find new and sustainable sources of income.

In order to do all that, or even to begin with a project apt to address each part of all that, Pope Leo XIV will need to undertake a reform of Roman curial culture. Cultural reform is the most difficult and dangerous kind of reform, especially when it is a reform of institutional culture. Whether Pope Francis learned this the hard way, or whether he had a hard time because he never really learned it, or whether he hardly learned the lesson of what we may call the first phase of his pontificate, is a matter for historians. What is certain is that he did not bequeath to his successor an institution or a leadership culture in form for action. On Francis' watch, the situation in the Holy See and the Vatican City State went from unsustainable to untenable. Laying the hopelessness of current arrangements before the public, thus making real reform action both morally and physically impossible to postpone, may well be credited to Francis as a great service.

In any case, regular and complete publication of balance sheets will go a long way toward building confidence among the faithful. That is a necessary, though not a sufficient step. Pope Leo XIV can lead by example in two regards. He can be completely forthright about the use of Peter's Pence money, relying on the goodwill of the faithful to support the Holy

See. In other words, Leo could—perhaps ought to—lean into the facts, rather than shy away from them or explain through surrogates how supporting the Holy See really is integral to the support of the Holy Father's mission in the world, which is a mission of charity. It is not wrong to say such things, but people know when they are being had, and they do not like it, even and especially when they cannot put their finger on precisely how they are being had.

Internationalizing the Roman Curia is something that could go a very long way toward improving both transparency and regularity of operations. Pope Benedict XVI had begun a process of extracting the Holy See's financial institutions from its virtual embedding in the Italian system, but much of the progress in that direction was undone during the Francis era, often in response to specific crises and scandals. In this regard, one thinks of the many permanent deacons ordained throughout the developed world, many of whom have decades of experience in finance, law, and business generally. Some of them could be persuaded to offer their services, especially if their work was apt to foster a new and transparent professional curial culture. There is even a sense in which a corps of deacons responsible for managing the temporal goods of the Holy See would be a return to tradition. The "seven deacons" of Rome (iconographically representing the original seven deacons chosen by the Apostles at Jerusalem, with each Roman deacon responsible for a geographical sector of the ancient imperial capital) go back to the fourth and even the third century.

The reality of the situation, in any case, is that Pope Leo XIV will need to trust the really independent expertise from individuals and institutions outside the Roman curial structure, whatever their state of life in the Church, while also improving morale among his already overworked and underpaid staff. In the current curial culture, management is top-down rather than consultative, siloed rather than collegial. Initiative is discouraged and occasionally punished. A 2022 survey conducted by the *Associazione Dipendenti Laici Vaticani*—the "Association of Lay

Vatican Employees" (not quite a union but the closest thing to one for Vatican employees)—reported an overwhelming majority of workers feel things have been getting worse.[90] If the Holy See is to avoid collapse under the weight of its own corruption and incompetence, it will need to get the very best from its people, and there is no squeezing blood from a stone.

It is precisely because of the enormous financial pressure facing the Holy See, that Pope Leo XIV must find the way to get the various departments of his government to abandon their silos and embrace real collaborative culture. That, in turn, will require a highly trained and flexible workforce, smaller in number than it is at present, not only capable but willing to do more with less. Leo will need to foster and harness, rather than suppress and dissipate their energies. The value of each employee in dollars and cents will only increase, but at present employees are not compensated at rates that reflect their importance to the operation. The current culture and configuration of the Holy See is ill-equipped for the challenge, to be perfectly frank, and time is running out.

Regarding new sources of income, the fact is that finding them is dicey. It takes money to make money, and the Holy See does not have a great deal of money. Licensing the papal likeness is something that could bring in some not insignificant revenue, but is usually dismissed out of hand as impossibly crass. In the 1990s, an Italian production company produced and sold a record of Pope John St. Paul II praying the rosary, which in part supported the *50 Chiese per Roma 2000* project—"50 Churches for Rome 2000"—an initiative of the Rome vicariate to repair and restore 50 churches in the city ahead of the great jubilee year 2000. St. John Paul II charted several times, in fact, beginning in 1979. Other popes have charted through the years, as well, from Pope St. John XXIII (in 1963) to Benedict XVI (multiple times, beginning in 2009), to Pope Francis (also multiple times). The popes lent their names and/or voices to those projects, however, often to support specific initiatives unconnected to the Holy See. There is no reason in principle why a Christmas album of the Sistine Chapel Choir, for example, shouldn't be an annual best-seller (there was a special Christmas album in 2017 and there have been other special recordings through the years), even if regular recordings of the pope praying the rosary or doing a sort of papal *Desert Island Discs* should be a bridge too far.

While individual figures, subsidiary institutions, and curial departments could find ways to defray their own operating costs (and even approach self-sufficiency), centralized control of the curial purse will likely discourage rather than encourage such initiatives. On the other hand, having each department maintain its own purse would—as it had in the past—encourage a culture of fiefdom in the curia, which cannot be conducive to coordinated operation and in fact reinforces the silo mentality. The problem is thorny, indeed. Really, it is an irreducibly complex set of problems, and action on any one of them will inevitably affect all the others. On 8 May 2025, the whole business became Pope Leo XIV's problem.

A long time coming

Peter's Pence, by the way, has its origins in the ninth century, through a pious initiative of England's King Alfred the Great. Western Europe was slowly recovering from the collapse of Roman power, and the papacy as an institution was developing along with the emerging realms that would become the states of Europe. In the vacuum created by the collapse of Roman power, the papacy came to take on the duties of civil government in central Italy. It was not long before popes were behaving like other secular rulers of the age.

In fairly short order, powerful central Italian crime families began to contend for the papacy as though it were their personal possession. Two families in particular, the Theophylacti and the Crescentii—both of which traced their origins to ancient Rome—contended for the papacy over the better part of a hundred years between the ninth and tenth centuries. In general, the Theophylacti preferred to hold the papal office directly, while the Crescentii preferred often enough to control the fellow who nominally held the office.

This period came to be known as the *saeculum obscurum*—the dark century—in which events like the infamous "cadaver synod" took place, i.e., the exhumation and posthumous trial of Pope Formosus under Pope Stephen VI, rather the opposite of an edifying affair, wrapped in broader Frankish and German political intrigues, as well as Roman familial quarrels. There were varying kinds and degrees of corruption and depravity during those years, but there was a very high turnover rate, and the prestige of the papal office was low, as was its moral stature. Leo VI, who reigned less than a year between June 928 and February 929, dealt with disputes over ecclesiastical jurisdictions in former imperial provinces, showing both the persistence of the vestiges of Roman order (sometimes sustained by Byzantine involvement in the former territories of the western empire) and the difficulty of governing through emergent institutions.

The whole history of the period is fascinating, and well worth a reader's time.[91] For now, suffice it to say that the Church and the papacy have been through some hard times before. The papacy will doubtless go through them again. There is a real and really important sense in which some serious thinking about how and where the current crisis facing the papacy fits into the whole broad sweep of the papal office's history. Ascertaining just exactly how the present moment stacks up against those earlier rough patches, however, is less important than understanding that the papacy is in another rough patch right now.[92]

It was the great ecclesiastical historian, Caesar Cardinal Baronius, who popularized the term, *saeculum obscurum*, in his seminal sixteenth-century work, *Annales Ecclesiastici*. Baronius began his *Annales* but did not finish the series. Oderic Raynaldus, a Roman nobleman and a priest of the then-recently founded Oratorian congregation (the Congregation of the Oratory, founded in 1575 by St. Philip Neri, who is sometimes called the "third apostle of Rome" after Saints Peter and Paul), completed the dozen volumes and brought them through to 1565. The great literary project was, in part, an answer to the Lutheran version of papal history captivating the imagination of European literati in those days. There is something of a lesson in that fact of history, as well. Frank and forthright acknowledgment of sins, errors, malfeasance, and general poor decision-making is always a better policy than defensive posturing, denial, and reaction.

The bottom line

The financial crisis is thorny, in short, because it requires urgent address and far-sighted leadership capable of building a viable structure in the long term. It is already a daunting task, and a sobering example of the truth articulated in the first chapter, about the practically achievable good, in essence that repairing a ship while underway is always difficult and dangerous. As we shall see in the chapter to follow, the financial crisis and the crisis of justice in the Church are really functions of one another. Addressing both will require great expense of time, effort, intellectual and spiritual energy, and money. The Church is not lacking in intellectual and spiritual wherewithal, though she does need to recover a sense of herself in history. Time and money, however, are two things in very short supply.

It is possible that an episode from the infancy of Pope Leo XIV's native United States could prove instructive: the XYZ Affair. In 1797, US President John Adams sent a three-man diplomatic mission to France with instructions to negotiate an end to rapacious French practices against US-flagged merchant vessels. Elbridge Gerry, John Marshall, and Charles Cotesworth Pinckney dealt with go-betweens, code-named in dispatches X (Jean-Conrad Hottinguer), Y (Pierre Bellamy), and Z (Lucien Hauteval), for Charles Maurice de Talleyrand-Périgord, the French foreign minister (and a Catholic bishop who had resigned the See of Autun and abandoned the exercise of his Holy Orders during the French Revolution). Through his intermediaries, Talleyrand demanded from the US diplomats as a condition of beginning negotiations. When the French agents' demands became known to the US public, furore and war fever ensued. "Millions for defence, but not one cent for tribute!" was the rallying cry in the American press.[93]

Pope Leo XIV may fairly hear and receive the diffidence of the worldwide body of the faithful as saying, "Millions for reform, but not one cent for business as usual!" Catholics have a right to good government, after all. They have a right to knowledge of the character and conduct of their rulers in the faith. They have a right to know how their money is being spent. Church leaders around the world have long acknowledged these rights in principle. It falls now to Leo, to make their undertakings his own and to make good on them in fact.

Here, too, the issue is one of internal discipline, but it is not merely one of internal Church discipline. It is a problem facing at once *ad intra* and *ad extra*. Catholics need to be able to trust their leaders with their money, or else they will simply stop giving to support the Church. This is especially true when it comes to the pope and the Holy See. If Church leaders cannot be trusted with temporal goods—the money and the assets the money acquires and maintains—the world will not be able to trust them when they proclaim Christ crucified and risen.

Chapter 8

Reform of justice

The images disappeared from the official Vatican News website without explanation, between 7 June and 8 June 2025—practically in the night between Saturday and Sunday—replaced with images of Christian artworks from other artists and periods, in a range of styles, on the pages of the Vatican's online liturgical calendar. There was no announcement of the changes, no indication that anything would be changing on the website. Once the changes had been made, there was no signal or attestation anything had been altered in the slightest. The changes, however, were big news. People all over the world had been clamouring for their removal, for well over two years.

Some early news reports credited Pope Leo XIV for the change. That was a reasonable surmise. The continued use of the images had been a matter of stated policy publicly articulated and defended by the head of the Vatican's own communications department, Dr. Paolo Ruffini, in 2024. So, the order to remove the images must have come from someone in a position to give it. More to the point, the order must have come from someone Ruffini and his dicastery would have to obey. The list of people in such a position is rather short.

Speaking on background—with rare notable exception, conversations for this book were backgrounders—one person with knowledge of the situation (perhaps channelling the ghost of the storied John Paul II-era Vatican press office director Joaquin Navarro-Valls) said, "No one could contradict" the assertion that Leo himself gave the order. In any case, the change came in the night, and quietly. If Leo ordered it, he did not say that he ordered it, let alone why he ordered it. "The world must construe according to its wits," Robert Bolt makes his Thomas More say in the climactic trial scene of his biographical drama, as it is beginning to appear the fix is in against the great English statesman and martyr, "this court must construe according to the law." No one is on trial over the offending images—not yet, as of this writing—but the ability of the Vatican to do justice on the author of the original works is very much at stake. That consideration must have informed Leo's decision to do things quietly and—one may surmise—to let actions speak for themselves.

The removal of the offending images was a major news development because the images were digital reproductions of pieces created by Fr. Marko Rupnik, a disgraced former Jesuit who had made quite a name for himself as a mosaic artist over the course of a career that spanned more than three decades. In the first week of December 2022, news reports began to carry gruesome allegations against Rupnik. Several people—dozens of victims would come forward, eventually—accused Rupnik of serial sexual, psychological, and spiritual abuse.

The Rupnik Affair, quite frankly, deserves its own book. It is an impossibly twisted, sordid, and thoroughly macabre tale, involving three generations of leadership in the Vatican, in the late pontiff's Jesuit order, and every pope from John Paul II to Leo XIV, though none more closely than Pope Francis. Rupnik escaped prosecution for a time, because the Congregation for the Doctrine of the Faith (now styled the Dicastery for the Doctrine of the Faith), which had found a case to answer, declared the charges against Rupnik statute barred. That decision did more than raise eyebrows when news of it reached the public—belatedly, in December 2022, and thanks primarily to Italian blog *Silere non possum* and Nicole Winfield of the Associated Press—since it also emerged around the same time that a secret Vatican court had convicted Rupnik, in 2020, of absolving an "accomplice" in a sexual sin, meaning the absolution of another person somehow involved in sexual sin with the absolving cleric. The secret tribunal secretly declared Rupnik excommunicated for that offence, then secretly (and very swiftly) lifted the secret excommunication.[94]

There was mountainous evidence against Rupnik already collected. There would have been ample opportunity for Rupnik to confront witnesses against him through counsel, if CDF had waived the statute bar (which it was in their power to do). There simply was no plausible reason for the decision not to lift the bar. Statutes of limitations exist to ensure fair trials. Rupnik could have received at least what passes for one at ecclesiastical law. The Society of Jesus—the Jesuits—expelled Rupnik in 2023, for disobedience (not for his crimes of abuse), after he flouted restrictions his erstwhile Jesuit superiors had placed on him. That made Rupnik a sort of "free agent" under ecclesiastical law, available to any diocese or religious congregation that would have him, though the prevailing wisdom was that Rupnik was radioactive.[95]

In the event, the Diocese of Koper in Rupnik's native Slovenia did accept him. In fact, Koper invited Rupnik to join their diocesan clergy. "Rupnik had not been sentenced to any judicial sentence," Koper's vicar general told *The Pillar*.[96] The implication was that, since Rupnik had not been convicted of any crime, he could keep good standing and the full exercise of his Holy Orders as a priest of the diocese. When that news reached the public, it sparked incandescent global outrage.[97]

Pope Francis never confirmed that he ordered the CDF/DDF not to lift the statute of limitations and bring Rupnik to trial. Francis did tell the Associated Press that he tends to leave such legal safeguards as statutes of limitations in place when cases of abuse involve victims who were not minors or vulnerable persons. How the victims of Marko Rupnik—most of them women religious who had been somehow in his spiritual care or under his authority—were not "vulnerable" in the legally pertinent sense, simply boggled everyone who knew the case or anything about it. In any event, it is certain that Francis did not waive the statute of limitations against Rupnik at first, and only waived it at last, in the wake of the sustained furore over news Rupnik had joined the clergy of Koper.

Pope Francis' precise role in the Rupnik Affair is only one major piece of a business appalling from start to finish, satisfactory explanation of which has not been so much as attempted.[98] Pope Francis died in April of 2025, nearly eighteen months after he lifted the statute of limitations and ordered the review of the Rupnik Affair. The prefect of the Dicastery for the Doctrine of the Faith, Cardinal Fernández, told reporters in March of 2025—mere weeks before Francis succumbed to his last illness—that his dicastery was still working to empanel judges capable of conducting the trial. When the cardinals elected Leo XIV, the case was still pending. It loomed over the conclave.

Leo XIV: Unfinished business

The unfinished business of the Francis pontificate—not only the Rupnik business—represents at once an urgent challenge and a precious opportunity to Pope Leo XIV, a trained canon lawyer with expertise and long experience as a judge in the Church's legal system. The challenge is urgent not only because the protracted global scandal of the Rupnik Affair is a microcosm of the larger crisis of clerical and hierarchical leadership culture in the global Church, but also because—fairly or no—the Rupnik business is a test case for Leo's governing acumen and commitment to justice. The same thing as makes the Rupnik case a challenge, also gives Leo the opportunity to begin the reform of ecclesiastical justice in earnest, with a win for Responsibility, Accountability, Transparency—a threefold watchword that became a bitterly ironic buzzword under Francis—while also salvaging some of the paper gains of the last quarter-century and perhaps something of his immediate predecessor's reputation. To accomplish all that—to accomplish any of that—Leo will have to thread a very narrow and very tricky needle.

Early indications were not the most promising. On 3 July 2025, Cardinal Fernández announced the judges had finally been chosen to try the case against Rupnik. Fernández explained that the judges selected were "all independent and external to our dicastery," the DDF, but he did not say who they were. "People were chosen who would not give rise to any suspicion," Fernández said. "The idea," he said, "was—if possible—to eliminate the idea that the Dicastery for the Doctrine of the Faith or the Holy See had any interest or were subjected to pressure." Fernández gave no indication of the specific charges against Rupnik, nor did he say whether a trial date had been set.

"There are technical times," Fernández told reporters, meaning the time it takes to accomplish certain necessary steps, "such as notification to the victims. We are working with the necessary confidentiality," Fernández said. Precisely what kind of confidentiality is necessary (and to what degree any should be necessary), indeed, the precise sense in which confidentiality should be necessary to the integrity of what is a public act concerning the public weal, is an open question at the heart of the problems facing the whole system of ecclesiastical justice. Given the notoriety of the Rupnik case and the highly publicized mismanagement of it, even a justice system in much better health than the Church's would be hard pressed to provide a fair trial.

Justice in a fallen world

In a perfect world, cases like that of Marko Rupnik would not happen. This world is not perfect. In a world marginally better than this, disasters like the Rupnik debacle would be fewer and farther between than they appear to be in fact. In an interview with Madrid's archdiocesan weekly *Alfa y Omega* magazine, published on 23 January 2025, Fernández said his dicastery has cases even more serious than Rupnik's. That statement was not news, in itself, but the impression it created was that the Rupnik business, despite its "complexity" and "delicacy"—words the head of DDF's discipline office, Archbishop John Kennedy, had used to describe the case[99]—was simply one among many.

Fernández was responding to a direct query from *Alfa y Omega* about the urgency of the need to resolve the Rupnik case. "In reality," Fernández answered, "I am thinking of many other cases, and some perhaps more serious [than Rupnik's] but less publicized." Sadly, that claim is not difficult to credit. The depths of wickedness are not fathomable, and most wickedness is of the workaday sort. Human nature is not only weak, but broken. Any Augustinian worth his salt will acknowledge the fact. One major challenge facing Pope Leo XIV, therefore, will be to balance requirements of justice: the claims and rights of victims, of the accused, and of the guilty; the protection of society; the punishment of evildoers.

Practical challenges: Justice as closeness to victims

A major source of trouble in the Vatican and in the Church more broadly is the confusion of the various kinds of response—cultural, legislative, executive, and judicial—necessary to address the persistent crisis of clerical and hierarchical leadership culture. They are all necessary. They are all related to one another. They are distinct, but not separate. Most important for the Church, they are all properly pastoral responsibilities of churchmen.

Church leaders, from popes down, have made much of the need for "closeness" to victims—and they are not wrong about that—but the one thing for which victims, their advocates, the faithful, and observers worldwide continue to clamour, is to see the Church do justice. Closeness to victims is as much a matter of letting justice be seen to be done, as it is about providing necessary spiritual, psychological, and basic human support to victims of clerical crime. It is a thorny issue, not least because it is very difficult to see precisely where the *What?* part of the business ends and the *How?* part begins. Justice, a public good, is a process.

The requirements of natural justice

In an address to Italy's National Association of Magistrates in the Jubilee Year 2000, Pope St. John Paul II described the judiciary power in a modern democratic state as one that "stands side by side with the legislative and executive powers," "having its own autonomous and constitutionally protected function." That description, however, applies as well to any well-ordered state and indeed any developed polity worth the name. The modern democratic systems are but one response to the requirements of natural justice. "A legal culture, a State governed by law, a democracy worthy of the name," as John Paul II put it in that same address, "are therefore characterized not only by the effective structuring of their legal systems, but especially by their relationship to the demands of the common good and of the universal moral principles inscribed by God in the human heart."

The Catholic Church is not a democracy. The Catholic Church, however, is a polity with a legal culture of its own. Indeed, the Catholic Church in both East and West has a venerable history of jurisprudence reaching back many centuries into antiquity, and an enviable tradition of legal scholarship that has been a carrier—sometimes the chief carrier—of the great achievements of law and legal culture generally. A legal culture as such—not regardless of its design, but prior to any consideration of its design—is characterized by its relationship to the demands of the common good. Justice, in other words, is by its very nature a public good. Those who administer justice do so in the name of the people over whom they rule, inasmuch as they administer in the name of the people's ruler.

This is true of the Church, of the bishops and the pope who are the rulers of God's people in the faith. In the Church's case, justice is done primarily for the people of God—the Catholic faithful and indeed all baptised Christians, howsoever subject to the Church's law—in the name of God and under his vicar, ultimately the pope. An independent judiciary is a requirement of natural justice, in other words, under any form of government or system of rule, whether civil or ecclesiastical. "[A]s there are on earth two principal societies, the one civil, the proximate end of which is the temporal and worldly good of the human race; the other religious, whose office it is to lead mankind to that true, heavenly, and everlasting happiness for which we are created," wrote Pope Leo XIII in his encyclical letter of 8 February 1884, *Nobilissima Gallorum gens*, "so these are twin powers, both subordinate to the eternal law of nature, and each working for its own ends in matters concerning its own order and domain." Leo XIII was writing in address of some very specific historical challenges then facing the people of France and the Church in France, in the context of world-historical socio-political disruption and upheaval, but his statement of principle—that both Church and State (or civil power, as he put it) are subordinate to the eternal law of nature—stands on its own. The judiciary must also—and therefore—be able to do its work "without fear or favour" as the old saying goes, which means the judiciary must not only possess the wherewithal to do justice but also be secure in its possession of that where-withal, or else whatever it does will not be justice at all.

Natural justice and judicial independence

From prehistoric hunter-gatherers to great imperial orders, the idea that judges must somehow be free to do their work—free, that is, of influence and pressure from private parties or other public powers—is present in human societies in some form or another. In short, the judiciary power in any articulate society—and the Catholic Church in the twenty-first century certainly is one of those—must be independent, not merely on paper but in fact. The independence of the judiciary, in turn, will be secure only when the judiciary is properly funded. The paper independence of the judiciary will be worthless for so long as judicial officials depend for their livelihoods solely or primarily upon the goodwill of a power external to their specifically judicial public purpose. The structures within which judicial officials work must be properly trained, staffed, and supported, as well. All that is more easily said than done.

Both of those requirements—judicial independence and effective empowerment—have vexed the Catholic Church for some time. The power structure of the Church is hierarchical, with one man at the top, who holds supreme, immediate, universal jurisdiction over the whole Church (effectively, all the twenty-two self-governing Churches in communion with Rome, and by divine law all Churches everywhere) and all the faithful. The pope, in other words, is the supreme governor of all Christians. He is not only the supreme legislator of the Church, but also the Church's chief executive and head judge. Also, judicial systems are expensive.

At present, the Discipline Section of the Dicastery for the Doctrine of the Faith employs a full-time staff of sixteen people. If one includes Archbishop John Kennedy, the long-serving and indefatigable Irishman who heads the Discipline section, there are seventeen people doing the work in an office with a worldwide remit. Discipline is responsible—either directly or indirectly—for nearly half a million clerics of various ranks serving in a global organization of some 1.4 billion members. The total annual DDF budget is roughly €3 million. A high-ranking source inside DDF speaking on background suggested Discipline accounts for somewhere between a quarter and a third of that total.

By contrast, public records show the annual judicial branch budget for the US State of Montana in 2024 to have been roughly $60 million. Montana's 2024 budget for the Department of Justice was just over $150 million. Montana's total area is 147,000 square miles and its total population is estimated at

1.14 million. Montana, it bears mention, has no general sales tax, very low property taxes, a progressive tax on personal income that runs between 4.7 and 5.9 per cent (and is one of a few states that allows residents to deduct a portion of federal income tax from their state returns), and a 6.75 per cent corporate income tax, making Montana the US state with the sixteenth lowest tax burden per capita and thirteenth lowest by percentage of income, with $5,185 in state and local debt per capita and 73 per cent funded ratio of public pension plans. [100]

2022 budget figures for the Holy See and Vatican City show total expenditures of €41 million for Apostolic Nunciatures, €38 million for communications, and €21million for the evangelisation dicastery. All other tribunals of the Holy See had a combined budget of €3 million, as well. There is a line in the Gospel according to St. Matthew: "For where thy treasure is, there is thy heart also." (Mt. 6:21) Pope Francis declared an "all-out battle" against abuse and cover-up in the Church, but neither Francis nor his predecessors prepared the Church for the fight. [101]

Reserve powers

The constitutional side of the matter is best framed as a question: How does one build an independent judicial system under one man with absolute power? Regarding the independence of the judiciary directly, it would doubtless require that the pope adopt and operate by a "reserve powers" doctrine not entirely dissimilar to the one by which the crown operates in the English state. The pope would have to hold power, in other words, without wielding it personally or officially. This is not a new idea, either among scholars or in the popular press. [102]

The history of English attempts at limiting royal power is not only centuries long, but seminal and foundational to the whole Western civilizational project, and indeed is the common patrimony of humanity. Pope Benedict XVI spoke to this in his historic address to Parliament in 2010. "This country's Parliamentary tradition owes much to the national instinct for moderation, to the desire to achieve a genuine balance between the legitimate claims of government and the rights of those subject to it," Benedict said. "While decisive steps have been taken at several points in your history to place limits on the exercise of power, the nation's political institutions have been able to evolve with a remarkable degree of stability," Benedict continued, noting how Britain emerged through that process "as a pluralist democracy which places great value on freedom of speech, freedom of political affiliation and respect for the rule of law," as well as strong sense of individuals' duties—hence their rights—and of all citizens' equality before the law. "While couched in different language," Benedict said, "Catholic social teaching has much in common with this approach, in its overriding concern to safeguard the unique dignity of every human person, created in the image and likeness of God," and in the emphasis Catholic social teaching places "on the duty of civil authority to foster the common good."

Some of those decisive steps, however, like the Glorious Revolution and the Hanoverian succession, have no historical analogue in the Catholic Church. They are not likely ever to find any analogue, for the simple reason that the primacy of the pope is divinely instituted. In other words, the Church is tightly limited in her ability to alter her own constitution, in a way the English and more broadly the British are not. In fact, the Catholic Church had its own centuries-long episode of discernment over this very question.

The conciliarist controversy and its aftermath

The conciliarist controversy, as it is known, was a protracted debate over whether the pope is the supreme power in the Church or whether an ecumenical council—a general gathering of all the world's bishops, the highest ordinary corporate organ of teaching and government in the Church, with roots in the so-called Council of Jerusalem recorded in Chapter 15 of the *Acts of the Apostles* and an unbroken practice since the first Council of Nicaea in AD 325—may rightly bind a pope or bend the pope to the conciliar will, either by thwarting the papal power or overriding the papal will. Conciliarists, of whom there were many of many different stripes, would have answered that question in the affirmative. Papalists would have answered it in the negative. In the event, the papalists won. That is the short and tidy version of a long and complex story. Conciliarism absorbed a great deal of energy from the fourteenth century to the sixteenth and was only finally put to rest—if really it ever has been put to rest—by the same Vatican Council I that dogmatically defined papal supremacy in 1870.

The Glorious Revolution, on the other hand, decisively gave Parliament supremacy over the crown. The Hanoverian succession—quite apart from its enshrining a prohibitive constitutional preference for Protestants over Catholics with otherwise powerful claims to the throne—not only confirmed Parliament's right to seat rulers, but led to significant further curtailing of royal activity in government. The English solution (which has its own downsides), is in any case unavailable to the Church, as a matter of historical fact ultimately rooted in the Church's divine constitution. Nevertheless, the "achieve[ment of] a genuine balance between the legitimate claims of government and the rights of those subject to it," as Benedict XVI put it, has been an open question in the Church for as long as there has been a Church at all. The history of the Catholic Church—in many ways, the whole history of Christianity in the world—is the story of the Church's very public and frequently maladroit attempts to strike that balance.[103]

Chapter 9

The nature and limits of papal governing power

The basic problem is twofold: of power and its articulation. The pope is supreme ruler of the Church. Under God, the pope's power is absolute. The pope's power, however, is neither limitless nor total. Other bishops, priests, men and women religious, and the lay faithful all have duties according to their baptism and state of life in the Church, which means they have rights, which the pope is bound to respect. Prior to that, every human being is a person with natural obligations, hence natural rights, regardless of baptism or status in the Church, which no power on Earth may deny, truncate, or unduly burden or abridge.

The pope's power comes from God, Catholics say, but it comes to the pope through the Church, for the government of which the papal office is given. The limits of papal power, therefore, are at once natural and political. Every power vested in a government includes the right to employ means fairly applicable to the purposes for which governing power as such is given, means in accord with the natural law and the essential ends of polity as such, and in keeping with the constitution of the society in and for which the governing power is erected. It happens that a Founding Father of Pope Leo XIV's native United States articulated the principle succinctly.

Governing power as such

"[E]very power vested in a government is in its nature sovereign," Alexander Hamilton put it in his 1791 opinion on the constitutionality of a national bank, "and includes, by force of the term, a right to employ all the means requisite and fairly applicable to the attainment of the ends of such power," provided those means are "not precluded by restrictions and exceptions specified in the [US] Constitution, or not immoral, or not contrary to the essential ends of political society." Hamilton went on to say the principle, "in its application to government in general, would be admitted as an axiom[.]" He was not wrong. "[I]t will be incumbent upon those who may incline to deny it," Hamilton continued, "to prove a distinction, and to show that a rule which, in the general system of things, is essential to the preservation of the social order, is inapplicable to the United States."[104]

If invoking Hamilton strikes a reader as strange, consider that Pope Leo XIV and Alexander Hamilton both belong to a very peculiar tradition of nationhood, which is that of the United States. Consider also that Hamilton, though he was applying it to the United States (in the infancy of US order under the Constitution that is still in force), was about the business of articulating a general principle. As a general principle, the one Hamilton effectively articulated in the context of a political debate (over the question whether the federal government could, in a manner consistent with the new Constitution, enact a law creating a national bank) is generally applicable. Substitute "the Catholic Church" for "the United States" and one is left not with the question whether the principle is valid in general, but whether the constitution of the Church provides any reason to except her from its application to her organs and structures of power.

At very least, it ought to be worth any reader's while to test the proposition against what is more certainly known of the theoretical limits to papal power. The pope may not order a man to sin, for example, or a bishop to impede or cause to cease any necessary care of his flock (though he may for grave reason depose bishops or place persons or jurisdictions under interdict, etc.). The pope must not unduly impede a Christian in the discharge of his duty under the natural law, or baptism, or according to that Christian's state of life in the Church. Within those broad confines—and they are very broad indeed—the pope is morally and constitutionally free to dispose of energies, to erect and to modify and amend, as well as to destroy organs and channels of power, according to his view of their aptness to service of purpose. There may be a compelling reason in fact, though there is no necessary reason discernible, why a pope may not erect a stable system of courts to administer justice in his name.

Justice in the ecclesiastical system

In fact, the Church already has such tribunals. What is needed is to make them materially capable, meaningfully accessible, transparent in their operations, and really independent. Achieving such a reform goal, or even beginning it well, would be a gargantuan undertaking. A functioning judicial system would require years to design and establish. It would require years—even a decade or more—to educate and train the class of professional jurists needed to manage caseload. Happily, the Vatican City state has already a system—a distinct civil system in the temporal order—which, for all its highly publicized troubles in recent years, has nevertheless provided the pope and the Church with proof-of-concept.

Several scandals have unfolded in and around the Vatican over the last twenty years, several of which have resulted in public trials at Vatican City criminal court. All of those trials, for all the legitimate criticism of the ways in which they were conducted and the reasons for which they were conducted at all, unfolded in view of the public. The charges were published. The verdicts were published, as well. Journalists had access to proceedings, rulings, judgments, and some—at least—of the evidence and the acts. Justice was done imperfectly, but it was seen to have been done.

By contrast, canonical tribunals do not publish charges.[105] Proceedings are not open to the public. Canonical processes both in the Vatican and at the diocesan and metropolitan levels are basically paper affairs.[106] Verdicts are reported in nebulous terms, if they are reported at all. Victims have limited rights of access to proceedings (such as they are), acts, filings, rulings, even verdicts (even after a 2021 reform of the universal law governing penal process at canon law).[107] The faithful have basically none.

In principle, the ideas of human dignity and natural justice, which Catholic social teaching applies to her thinking about civil authority, are not limited to civil government. In practice, senior churchmen too often think—to judge by their behaviour and their justifications for it—of the Church herself as a special case, exempt in practice from her own social doctrine. Said bluntly, ecclesiastical justice ought to exceed the minimum natural requirements and be an exemplar for civil jurisdictions, but systematically fails her own test in these regards. This state of affairs has never really been sustainable. It has long since become untenable.

The secrecy of trials at canon law has destroyed the confidence of both clerics and the faithful, who do not trust in the Church's ability to deliver justice. What is worse, secrecy causes candid minds both within and without the Church to doubt the *bona fides* of the whole institution in matters pertaining to the administration of justice. The addiction to secrecy rightly gives great pause as well, therefore, to Christians generally and to others who might otherwise approach the Church for wisdom, succour, fellowship, and even for membership. In a word, the Church's addiction to secret process is a scandal, in the strict technical sense of the term; a stumbling block.[108]

Twin challenges: transparency and judicial independence

Developing a meaningfully public judicial culture within the canonical system will not be easy, but the judicial system of the

Vatican City State incontrovertibly demonstrates that secrecy is neither a requisite for the fair treatment of churchmen nor a requirement of natural justice. Several trials at Vatican City criminal court—a civil jurisdiction, you will recall, within the Vatican City State—have incontrovertibly demonstrated that meaningfully public trials even of clerics accused of sex crimes and cover-up is possible. The 2021 Martinelli case, in fact, did just that. Two defendants faced charges, which were published and tried before a public that included journalists, in several stages, between 2021 and 2024.[109]

Don Gabriele Martinelli was accused of abusing another student, identified as L.G. in court documents, over a five-year period, 2007–12, when they were both students at the St. Pius X Pre-Seminary, then located inside the Vatican. After a protracted and highly imperfect process that nevertheless involved the testimony of several very senior churchmen including Angelo Cardinal Comastri (who was Vicar General of Vatican City and President of the Fabric of St. Peter's Basilica at the time Martinelli was alleged to have committed his crimes), Martinelli was convicted on the charge of "corrupting a minor" and sentenced to two and a half years in prison. Don Enrico Radice, the rector of the minor seminary at the time of Martinelli's crimes, was charged with accessory crimes for his involvement—in essence, prosecutors claimed Radice had worked to discredit L.G.'s allegations—but ultimately found not guilty.

Given these facts, there cannot be any compelling reason in principle for which trials at canon law ought not also be meaningfully public. Justice, after all, is a public good. The people in whose name the organs of government conduct the machinery of justice have a right to know what the officers are doing in their name. This is a basic requirement, without which there is not even the semblance of justice. The creation of a real canonical criminal court system would require significant expense of material and intellectual capital, but need not be from scratch. The great thing will be to secure the means by which to guarantee that trials and other proceedings become and remain meaningfully public, and judges—the whole system—be protected from executive and other interference.

Secrecy untenable

The rationale for judicial secrecy in the ecclesiastical system (and elsewhere) is that it protects both accusers and the accused, while it is also supposed to safeguard the integrity of the judicial process by keeping the work of justice away from the baleful effects of exposure to public opinion. Hard experience, however, teaches how implausible is that rationale.[110] Even if the rationale for judicial secrecy were far more plausible than it is in general, the secret conduct of notorious cases—like Rupnik's, for example—is always deleterious and a recipe for disaster. It has long since become painfully apparent not only that the opacity of ecclesiastical processes may protect the guilty, but also how secrecy harms the innocent. The governors of the Church must see that allegations of abuse and cover-up are investigated, but the current practice of temporarily removing accused clerics during secret preliminary investigations, the findings of which are not published even in the event they lead to trial or the prospect of formal charges, contributes to permanent suspicion that looms over clerics investigated and officially cleared of wrongdoing. The practice of offering accused clerics the opportunity to escape trial by voluntarily petitioning for dismissal from the clerical state likewise serves to obscure the full extent not only of guilt but of the persistent danger a bad actor may pose to society at large.[111]

This standardised abuse of prosecutorial discretion has a deleterious effect on clerical morale and is dangerous to the public at large. Judicial secrecy, meanwhile, erodes confidence not only in leaders' ability to deliver justice but in their concern with delivering justice at all.[112] This is true for ecclesiastical as well as civil justice. There is a reason Lord Hewart's famous phrase has become a maxim: "Justice must be seen to be done."[113]

The Catholic Church has thousands of canonists already at work in her tribunals and chanceries. The overwhelming majority of them are capable, diligent, and honest (sometimes very nearly to the point of scrupulosity). To speak with them privately is to hear how well they know the inadequacies of the system in which they serve, and to learn how keenly they feel the press. Were every canon lawyer a St. Raymond of Peñafort and every ecclesiastical judge a St. Ives, the current system of ecclesiastical justice would still be manifestly untenable.

What could Pope Leo XIV do?

It bears mention here that Pope Leo XIV could order certain straightforward and common-sense steps almost immediately. The publication of charges would be one thing. The publication of verdicts would be another. In general, the publication of judicial acts, opinions, rulings, etc., would not be difficult. There are already practices stably in place in civil jurisdictions for the protection of persons—names, addresses, etc.—readily adaptable to ecclesiastical systems.

One key change would be to make judges hold their commissions securely during good behaviour. That would require modification of existing structural law in two directions, one to make it so judges cannot be removed without their consent except by impeachment and public trial, another to create the oversight and disciplinary mechanism required to make such an arrangement effective. Judges (and their staffs) would also require compensation to be drawn from a fund secured beyond the ordinary reach of the pope (or local bishop or metropolitan or conference). Ecclesiastical judges already act in the name of the pope—or the bishop or archbishop—as judges in England and other civil jurisdictions act in the name of the crown or the state or the federal or national government, or of the people. The next step is to secure ecclesiastical judges against the encroachments of the executive, while also making them answerable to a distinct power for official misbehaviour.

Lord Hewart, it bears mention, also wrote *The New Despotism*, published in 1929. A powerful and powerfully influential polemical tract, *The New Despotism* attacked the encroachments of the executive power on the other branches of government, amounting to usurpation of their powers tending "to render the will, or the caprice, of the executive unfettered and supreme." Candid minds must admit that the concentration of supreme executive, legislative, and judicial power in a single person tends rather to magnify and exacerbate than to attenuate the ills of an executive unchecked. "The old despotism, which was defeated, offered Parliament a challenge. The new despotism, which is not yet defeated, gives Parliament an anaesthetic." That line was from *The New Despotism* as well. It referred to the peculiar history of England, specifically to a trend the author saw as a dangerous encroachment of one power—the Executive—on another. On Hewart's view, the achievements of British constitutional order—achievements Benedict XVI had praised in his historic 2010 address to Parliament—were threatened by what he perceived to be a serious encroachment of the Executive. Ultimately at stake was the duty to safeguard human dignity and foster the common good, which Catholic social teaching rightly recognizes as among the essential ends of government as such, in every age.

The reform herein contemplated, in its extent and in its form, necessarily entails great expense of money and energy. False starts and missteps are inevitable and will come at surprising and inconvenient moments. Some of them will be very costly. Leaders will make mistakes, as will the faithful and the rank-and-file professionals called to definite service. It is nevertheless unequivocally evident that the status quo is not only unsustainable but untenable, that half-measures, excuses, and various postponements have been aggravating already dire circumstances for some time.

In any case, publicizing the results of a process without publishing the charges, and without conducting the process itself meaningfully in view of the public, destroys the public trust upon which confidence in the administration of justice entirely relies. That confidence is an indispensable bulwark of credible leadership. People who may be subjected to such travesties of justice—clerics not least, as they are far more likely than others to feel such power practiced upon themselves, especially those of the lower ranks—have every reason to fear those who wield such power. They have no reason to trust that anyone who wields such power should really be interested in the substance of justice. In such an environment, with such a recent history, it will be difficult for Pope Leo XIV and his people to convince either the faithful or the broad public of their earnest regarding responsibility, accountability, and most of all transparency.

Preliminary indications: theory and practice

Pope Leo XIV has already shown himself conversant with the tradition of thinking-in-public—what the late Alasdair MacIntyre has called a tradition of enquiry—in which the ideas informing the foregoing summary have their home. As an Augustinian, Leo is steeped in that tradition. In an address to the International Parliamentary Union on 21 June 2025, Leo explicitly invoked the idea of natural law as the lodestar of government and of governors. "Natural law, which is universally valid apart from and above other more debatable beliefs," Leo said, "constitutes the compass by which to take our bearings in legislating and acting, particularly on the delicate and pressing ethical issues that, today more than in the past, regard personal life and privacy." In that same address, Leo also spoke of the natural law as "an essential reference point," one "written not by human hands, but acknowledged as valid in all times and places, and finding its most plausible and convincing argument in nature itself," including human nature, in accord with which governors must always exercise their power, for the upbuilding of human community and the achievement of true human flourishing.

For the Augustinian, this means a twofold mindfulness: of our having been made in the image and likeness of God; of our fallen nature. Governors who forget one or the other are doomed to disastrous failure, the disaster directly proportional to their technical prowess and administrative competence. This is true of governments as well as of governors. Governments also put the societies over which they are erected in form for action in history.[114] Governments operate best when they conform to what Montesquieu called the "genius" and "circumstances" of the people over whom they are erected.[115]

The genius and circumstances of the Catholic Church are peculiar, indeed, but the Catholic Church is nonetheless a society, a polity, albeit one ordered to a supernatural end. The existential necessities of the polity that is the Catholic Church, therefore, are neither solely nor exclusively those of the natural order. Neither the divine constitution of the Church nor the supernatural orientation of ecclesiastical society broadly considered, however, may replace or supplant or otherwise abridge the natural law. The pope stands at the head of the Church's hierarchical communion as the supreme, though not the only ruler in the faith, and all who hold power in the Church are bound to respect certain rights of nature inhering in each and every human person, as well as the rights inhering in certain persons according to baptism and state of life in the society that is the Church.

Bishops in their own dioceses have powers and rights of government similar in kind, given for the same reasons and pursuant to like ends, differing primarily in scope. It would be both costly and time-consuming for diocesan bishops—local ordinaries in general—to build the systems and foster the juridical culture necessary to sustain them. The question facing local ordinaries, however, is not whether they can afford it. The question is whether they can afford not to undertake any such project.

As a practical matter, then, the pope could lead by example in these regards. He could commit to holding his powers in reserve, only he would have to honour his commitment even—and especially—when to do so were inconvenient. In order to be successful, he would require a cohort of judges and jurists trained and experienced, staffed and funded, far greater in number than anything of which the popes have heretofore disposed. It may also require an independent investigative arm, also properly trained, staffed, and funded, capable of conducting really independent inquiries subject to meaningful public scrutiny.

An investigative arm

Another major reform, therefore, could be the creation of just such an investigative arm, somewhat after the manner of a Department of Justice. Clerics and laity specially trained in the proper conduct of criminal investigations would work as full-time professionals. They could train local diocesan investigators and assist on an as-needed basis with material resources and human expertise. The investigative arm could be given primary jurisdiction over certain kinds of cases by universal law, e.g., cases involving multiple dioceses, or involving either religious clerics or religious orders, which are not always easily reached by local Ordinaries.

The investigative arm would have to be financially independent. It would have a say in its budget, which would come from funds put beyond the ordinary reach of other ecclesiastical power. The investigative arm would also need to function under competent oversight provided by an office or commission likewise independent of ordinary power. The oversight organism would in turn require a staff of professional legal and accounting experts, as well as persons with significant background in civil service and business.

Such an investigative arm could be organized in different ways. In many European civil jurisdictions, for example, investigators answer to a judge-investigator. In many other places, an office not unresembling the US Attorney General. In England and Wales, it is the Secretary of State for Justice or the Lord Chancellor or the Crown Prosecution Service. In the ecclesiastical sphere, one may reasonably expect such a figure to be a Prefect at the level of the Roman Curia and a Special Vicar or the like at the diocesan and metropolitan (i.e., archdiocesan) level. The key thing is that any such investigative arm, however organized, would publish the findings and results of its investigations. The arm would do this as a matter of course.

A metropolitan archbishop possessed of both moral and material wherewithal might on his own undertake to erect and establish such an arm within his province, even without Roman leadership. The opportunity of Roman leadership-by-example in these regards is nevertheless apparent. Once erected and established in Rome, metropolitans would have an easier time of it. Bishops' conferences—the stable corporate and administrative expressions of episcopal presence and action in countries and sometimes broad geopolitical regions—could marshal and dedicate resources for the support of investigative arms at every level. The lay faithful as well should participate actively and responsibly in the work of investigation and oversight. The laity—and universities, especially Catholic universities—could also provide auxiliary services covering a host of necessary areas, whether technical-scientific, counselling, direct professional oversight, regular and forensic accounting, *inter alia*.

Design of any system apt stably to serve the common good in these regards and thereby to earn the general trust, will doubtless require broad consultation. Persons in every state of life in the Church—laity, religious men and women, diocesan clerics of every rank—would need to contribute time and talent to the work. The expertise of persons from disparate fields and every walk of life would be not only healthy but necessary for success: lawyers and judges and even politicians, and also engineers and IT specialists, and people with experience managing projects and teams of all different sizes and personnel configurations, and doctors and psychological counsellors, and even plumbers and first-responders and medical doctors. In a word, such an effort would require the participation of practical problem-solvers with proven experience in the real world, all working together to resolve what is, at bottom, a real, practical, nuts-and-bolts problem of governance.

A Matter for the Synod of Bishops?

Properly organized and executed, an Extraordinary Assembly of the Synod of Bishops could be the very thing for sparking such a consultation on the universal level. Diocesan synods and diocesan synod assemblies held at regular intervals could facilitate not only the erection of investigative arms and oversight bodies fit for purpose and suited to local culture and custom, but also generally contribute to the upbuilding of common life of the Church and society. Pope Leo XIV could order the establishment of such diocesan bodies and stipulate that they should meet at regular intervals, in universal law. By using the Synod of Bishops, amending universal law, and empowering reform efforts at the local level, Leo could also—and at the same time—give institutional expression and stability to something that remained inchoate throughout the Francis pontificate.

There is, in fact, a great deal Pope Leo XIV (or any pope) could do to strengthen local and regional organs of ecclesiastical power. Until fairly recently, in fact, Metropolitan Archbishops—who are called such because they are in charge of an archdiocese, i.e., a jurisdiction with other dioceses (and their bishops) subordinate to the metropolitan in some respects of discipline and governance—have not only enjoyed on paper but really exercised power over their subordinates, called "suffragans" in ecclesiastical jargon. More recently, most of the metropolitan's historical oversight and disciplinary authority has been either returned to the local bishops over whom he has nominal authority, or else absorbed by Rome and ultimately the pope.

Making the *pallium* mean something (again)

It is interesting to note that the symbol of metropolitan authority in the Church is the *pallium*, the band of white lamb's wool with six black crosses embroidered that sits like a wide collar on the shoulders, which metropolitan archbishops in both East and West have certainly worn in one form or another since the eighth century as their peculiar sign of office (and connection to the Roman pontiff). For many centuries, it was necessary that a man appointed or elected to a metropolitan see receive his *pallium* before he exercised the powers of his office. More recently—very recently, indeed, in the life of an institution that thinks in centuries—Pope St. John Paul II ordered that new metropolitans should not only receive the *pallium* but have it imposed upon them directly by the pontiff during a special ceremony on the Solemnity of Saints Peter and Paul in Rome. Then, in 2015, Pope Francis decided that he would send the *pallia* to new archbishops and have the nuncio—the papal ambassador—impose it in a special local ceremony.

"The meaning of this change," explained the papal Master of Ceremonies at the time, then-Monsignor Guido Marini, in a 29 January 2015 interview with Vatican Radio, "is to put more emphasis on the relationship of the metropolitan archbishops – the newly nominated – with their local Church," and was to be seen as part of "that journey of synodality in the Catholic Church which, from the beginning of his pontificate, [Francis] has constantly emphasized as particularly urgent and precious." The change was, in other words, a gesture meant somehow to convey the sense informing Francis' programmatic thought and action in respect of synodality. As Charles Collins put it in a 12 June 2025 analysis piece for *Crux*, "The move of the imposition of the pallium from Rome to the home archdioceses of the archbishops was one of the first official acts concerning one of Pope Francis's key programs." That is why it was news when Pope Leo XIV announced he would be restoring the imposition of the pallium to the Mass marking the Solemnity of Saints Peter and Paul.

By using the Synod of Bishops as a catalyst for broad public conversation practically ordered to the wholesale reform of the ecclesiastical justice system, Pope Leo XIV could kill two birds with one stone. He could show how the Synod of Bishops established by Pope St. Paul VI and used by every pope since its establishment as either a talking shop or a rubber stamp or both, can be genuinely useful as a consultative body even without deliberative or other power. At the same time and by the same token, Leo could therein and thereby generate practical and actionable ideas for specific reforms, however in a safe and controlled environment. Leo could, in other words, answer the question that has vexed everyone in the Church, Francis included, for more than a dozen years: Is synodality in essence the legislative body characteristic of Eastern ecclesiastical polity (the powers of which have been largely absorbed in the West by the pope); or is synodality really only an expansion of the talking shop that is the Synod of Bishops established in the wake of Vatican II?

If some of the foregoing considerations appear to be at loggerheads with this observer's earlier suggestion, i.e., that Pope Leo XIV essentially restored the Synod of Bishops to factory settings, then consider that such restoration could well prove the first step toward real institutional reform of the Synod of Bishops as well as an answer to the *vexata quaestio* of synodality and a way toward a project of reform apt to put the ecclesiastical justice system in form for twenty-first-century action. Consider as well, that Leo's evident re-dimensioning of the General Secretariat of the Synod of Bishops in its present constitution and configuration is one thing, while the general fitness for purpose of the Synod as an institution is quite another. In any case, the primary purpose of all these considerations is not to advise on specific reform measures, much less to dictate policy, but to give a sense of the scope of reform required to address the problems of ecclesiastical justice. If Leo can convince churchmen of the need for reform on anything like the scale herein proposed, he will have achieved something mighty, regardless of the specifics.

★★★★★

Conclusion

Drivers of crisis

As I write these lines of conclusion to what has been a whirlwind adventure in composition, even for a wizened old hack like me, I think of Pope Leo XIV recently returned from his July holiday at the papal summer residence in Castel Gandolfo. His decision to leave town grabbed headlines, but it did not keep them. His presence in the ancient hill town delighted residents for reasons not solely spiritual. By the time this book is printed and bound, both his stay in the town and his return will be ancient history by the standards of the day. Summer will be giving way to autumn by the time it reaches sellers' shelves. I wonder what the fall and winter will have brought by the time this book is in your hands.

Morto un papa, se ne fa 'n' artro, as the Romans say, "When one pope dies, another is made." The making of Leo XIV was not a perfectly uncomplicated matter, and his pontificate will have to wrestle with converging crises driven by an inveterate inability to address the cultural motors of abuse and cover-up, general governance, a loss of the Church's own sense of history, and a leadership culture that is sclerotic if not necrotic, all at a time in which general confidence in political and social institutions is lower than it has been in generations and powerfully disruptive technological forces are at work in the world.

The election of Pope Leo XIV did not thrill me as had the elections of his predecessors. That was not because I did not think highly of him. It was because I knew more and better than I had in 2005 and 2013, about how great and terrible is the work before him. *Dulce bellum inexpertis.*

There has been some chatter over his early appointments, but most of those were already in the works before he came to the office. Leo was a steady presence through his first months, but those were the slow months in any case. There is always a great deal of movement beneath the surface in the Vatican, and one expects it to erupt sooner or later. This work—the work of observing, recording, and explaining the times—demands not prolepsis but clairvoyance. One must see clearly what is happening now.

More prosaically, I have observed how emerging technologies have eroded the space and polluted the climate of discourse, not only in the Church but certainly among Christians and particularly among Catholics, who are—after all—citizens along with everyone else, and people, hence cultural creatures. I have lamented many of the changes—a sign of my age, no doubt, but not merely a sign of that—and I have participated in the erosion and pollution, I am sure (though I do not believe it a delusion when I say I have done my level best not to). To the extent I have offered ideas as may help navigate the troubled waters of the present, I can only say that I tried to avoid giving advice, but only endeavoured to say what I have seen and continue to see. That is the work of a journalist, after all, who ought to say what he sees (and then be ready to take the hits as they come).

I want Pope Leo XIV to do well. I wanted Francis to do well, and Benedict XVI before him. I recall wondering whether I had prayed enough for Benedict when he resigned, and decided I had not. I am sure I did not pray enough for Francis while he reigned, though I remember fondly and with gratitude how he encouraged popular devotion, and must credit his invitation to daily and attentive prayer of the rosary in October 2018 with rekindling Marian devotion in me, which had become rather lax and perfunctory. It strikes me as oddly fitting, that I have written a book about a pontificate at its beginning, and these are heady days for sure.

"Faced with cultural changes throughout history," Pope Leo XIV told thousands of Catholic "digital missionaries" and "influencers" gathered in St. Peter's Basilica on 29 July 2025, "the Church has never remained passive; she has always sought to illuminate every age with the light and hope of Christ by discerning good from evil and what was good from what needed to be changed, transformed, and purified." Leo noted the ubiquitous presence of technology in the world and in our lives, especially the emergence and increasingly diffuse adoption of artificial intelligence marking a new era in human history. "This is a challenge that we must face," he said, "reflecting on the authenticity of our witness, on our ability to listen and speak, and on our capacity to understand and to be understood."

"We have a duty to work together to develop a way of thinking," Pope Leo XIV said, "to develop a language, of our time, that gives voice to Love." This is not a mere matter of generating content, "but of creating an encounter of hearts," Leo continued, which "will entail seeking out those who suffer, those who need to know the Lord, so that they may heal their wounds, get back on their feet and find meaning in their lives." Leo said that work "begins with accepting our own poverty, letting go of all pretence and recognizing our own inherent need for the Gospel. And this process is a communal endeavour."

"Go and mend the nets," Leo told his guests, an allusion to the episode in the Gospel according to Saint Matthew, in which the Lord calls the first disciples, James and John, as they were mending their fishing nets. It was a call not to leave work and follow, but to take it up in earnest, to be ready, to foster "networks of relationships, of love, of gratuitous sharing where friendship is profound and authentic," and "mend what has been broken, heal from loneliness, not focus on the number of followers, but experience the greatness of infinite Love in every encounter."

Perhaps the most powerful, and powerfully telling, lines of Pope Leo XIV's address were those inviting his guests to craft "networks that give space to others more than to ourselves, where no 'bubble' can silence the voices of the weakest." He described them further as "networks that liberate and save;

networks that help us rediscover the beauty of looking into each other's eyes; networks of truth." It was bracing, stirring rhetoric. He began his speech: "In the name of the Father, of the Son, and of the Holy Spirit, peace be with you!" Even reading it, I was transported to the *loggia* on that first evening.

The pontificate of Leo XIV is only just beginning. It will not be smooth sailing. There are too many crises facing the Church and society for it to be anything other than fraught with danger and adventure. There is no guarantee he will do well.

Un papa grasso ne segue uno magro, is another Roman saying, "A fat pope follows a thin pope." It is not so much a reference to physical stature, as it is to the different ways popes reign and rule. Pope Francis ruled, but he eschewed the trappings of reign. Francis was a thin pope. Leo XIV has retrieved many of the trappings his predecessor put away, but he will have to rule the Church sooner or later. When he does, the record of leadership he will make for himself shall be as amenable to criticism as that of any other world leader.

Catholics trust in the Lord's promise to bring the barque of Peter safely home. He makes no promises regarding how well or poorly she will be captained while she is underway, nor regarding the state she in which she will be when at last she comes to port. That the seas on which she travels are stormy, is certain. They always have been, more or less. Now, we discover of what seamanship this new lion of three worlds is capable. Leo XIV is pope now.

Notes

1 See "The one who goes into the conclave a pope, comes out a cardinal" by Christopher R. Altieri in *Catholic World Report*, 26 April 2025.

2 See "Challenges facing the conclave" by Christopher R. Altieri in *Catholic World Report*, 30 April 2025.

3 In the closing chapter of the 2024 edition of *The Wiley Blackwell Companion to Catholicism*, I put the matter roughly as one of muddling through that frequently looks and feels a lot like muddling about. See "Challenges for the Catholic Church" by Christopher R. Altieri in *The Wiley Blackwell Companion to Catholicism*, Frederick C. Bauerschmidt, James J. Buckley, Jennifer Newsome Martin, Trent Pomplun, eds., John Wiley & Sons, Ltd., 2024.

4 See "Reform Your Expectations of Church Reform" by Christopher R. Altieri in *Catholic Answers* (online), 23 September 2021.

5 Cf. Augustine of Hippo, *Confessiones* I.1: *quia fecisti nos ad te et inquietum est cor nostrum, donec requiescat in te*. The text of the *Confessions* is widely available electronically and in print, in Latin and in English and other vernacular translations. It has been in circulation for more than 1,600 years, never out of print since there has been the printing press. High school students read the book because it is a compelling story of a soul on a great adventure, scholars mine it, Christians bathe in it devotedly. The *Confessions* is the first literary autobiography, a genre Saint Augustine of Hippo may fairly be said to have invented. I am no expert on the book, but there were years between my late adolescence and early adulthood in which I

read in it almost daily and was almost never without a copy of it on my person.

6 Cavell offered that description in the opening remarks of his Tanner Lectures on Human Values at Stanford University in April of 1986. Cavell published them in a delightful book—a collection of lectures delivered at various places during the 1980s—titled *In Quest of the Ordinary*, with the University of Chicago Press, in 1988. Cavell's introduction to his Tanner Lectures explained his indebtedness to the influential twentieth-century philosopher, Martin Heidegger, for the phrase—"the uncanniness of the ordinary"—which became the title for his Lectures and a chapter of the aforementioned book. The significance of this for our subject is to be found, among other places, in the Augustinian constitution of Heidegger's magnum opus, *Being and Time*, articulated and defended in *Being and Conversion: A phenomenological ontology of radical restlessness*, the 1995 doctoral dissertation of Prof. Craig J.N. De Paulo at the Pontifical Gregorian University. De Paulo, it happens, is also a graduate of Villanova University (he and Leo did their undergraduate work there, though not at the same time) and was my teacher.

It is a very small world, after all, and also a very big world.

Saint Augustine's articulation of the structure of human experience—of the human experience of our own nature, which is the sense of our own being lost-and-found to ourselves and our fellows, divided against ourselves in what so often feels and appears to be a vain attempt to achieve whole-heartedness—is compelling precisely because it captures and discloses our selves to our selves, and in so doing, attunes us to the quiet and secret work of our Author.

7 Every once in a while, we may catch a moment in which, "[L]ife," as the great American storyteller (and professor of English literature at the University of Chicago) Norman Maclean once put it, "instead of going sideways, backwards, forward, or nowhere at all, lines out straight, tense and inevitable, with a complication, climax, and, given some luck, a purgation, as if life had been made and not happened." Intimations of that sort may come rarely. On the other hand, it may be that they are there for us always, but we are not well attuned to them. "The world is charged with the grandeur of God," says Gerard Manley

Hopkins SJ. The world is charged, I have always taken the line to suggest, as a pile is charged and also as a felon is charged. (Those who are interested will find the Maclean quote in his story, "USFS 1919: The Ranger, the Cook, and the Hole in the Sky" in *A River Runs Through It and Other Stories*, first published by the University of Chicago Press in 1976. The Hopkins line comes from "God's Grandeur" and is widely available online, but first appeared in *Poems of Gerard Manley Hopkins*, the 1918 volume of Hopkins' work posthumously published by the poet's friend and fellow poet, Robert Bridges).

8 Later in his *Confessions*, discussing the crucial turn into a life of divine and Catholic faith, Saint Augustine put the matter—if it were possible—even more starkly:

> *I*—while I was deliberating whether I should serve the Lord my God as long I had disposed [myself] to do—*I* was the one who was willing, [and] *I* was the one who was unwilling. Neither was I willing fully nor was I fully unwilling. I was contending with myself, therefore, and I was being lost to myself [literally "dissipated from myself"] and this self-same dissipation was surely working me against my will; though it did not show the nature of an alien mind but rather the pain [*poena*, lit. "punishment"] of my own. And so, it was not, therefore, *I*, who was working this, but the sin that abided in me, on account of the punishment [*supplicium*] of a sin more freely chosen, for *I* was a son of Adam. (*Conf.* VIII.x.22)

9 The CYMCAC was the precursor institution to Roosevelt University, arguably most famous as the *alma mater* of Chicago's first African-American mayor, Harold Washington. A WWII veteran who served as an enlisted soldier in the US Army Air Corps, Washington was a lawyer and Methodist minister, and among Chicago's first major African-American political figures to participate in the institutional life of the city's Democratic Party.

10 The history of the 1980 concordat between the Holy See and the Republic of Peru is not only interesting in its own right, but telling of the Holy See's political savvy and diplomatic acumen. In 1980, Peru was on the cusp of return to democracy

after a dozen years of military rule. The last of Peru's military rulers, General Francisco Morales Bermúdez, bowed to political pressure and economic reality at home to allow the drafting of a new constitution and then relinquished power, but participated with some alacrity in US-led intelligence programmes for the disruption, suppression, and—sometimes—elimination of left-wing political forces and figures throughout South America. The Holy See reached its agreement with his junta, thus guaranteeing the institutional position of the Church in Peru through the periods of transition and significant upheaval that followed.

11 See "Bridge Builder (How Robert Prevost became Leo XIV)" by Austen Ivereigh in *Commonweal*, 25 May 2025.

12 See "Peruvians know him as the priest who went 'from Chicago to Chiclayo.' He is now Pope Leo XIV" by Regina Garcia Cano and Franklin Briceño for the Associated Press, 9 May 2025.

13 See "She worked with Pope Leo XIV in Peru. Here's how she remembers him before his rise" by Adriana Gallardo for NPR: *Morning Edition*, 9 May 2025.

14 The *Chicago Sun-Times* originally reported the story on 26 February 2021, shortly after Pope Francis named then-Bishop Prevost of Chiclayo to the Congregation for Bishops (as it was then styled), but two years before Francis made Prevost the Prefect of the Dicastery for Bishops (the same department, renamed in the 2022 overhaul of the Roman Curia). Led by *The Pillar*, an independent investigative journalism project, Catholic outfits picked up the story. See "Church officials OK'd moving another priest accused of abuse to Hyde Park friary, records show" by Robert Herguth in *Chicago Sun-Times*, 26 February 2021. See also "Vatican congregation member allowed priest accused of child abuse to live near Catholic school" staff report in *The Pillar*, 16 March 2021.

15 See "Ex-priest accused of molesting kids says future Pope Leo XIV OK'd his move near South Side school" by Robert Herguth and Kaitlin Washburn in *Chicago Sun-Times*, 20 May 2025.

16 See "Vatican expert sees progress on abuse, but also resistance in some 'quarters'" by Beth Griffin for the Catholic News Service in *America Magazine*, 28 April 2019.

17 See "Pope Leo XIV: What we know already (and what we can expect)" by Christopher R. Altieri in *Crux*, 11 May 2025.

Pope Leo XIV also faced other allegations of mismanagement, stemming from his tenure as Bishop of Chiclayo. Those allegations faced careful vetting by the press, Peruvian civil authority, and the Vatican, and resulted in Prevost's complete exoneration. See "Serious questions of credibility surround cover-up allegations against new pope" by Elise Ann Allen in *Crux*, 9 May 2025.

18 The Greek original for "Peace be with [all of] you," is Εἰρήνη ὑμῖν, but the Greek readily translates the Aramaic (*Shlama Aleykhu*), which sounds a lot like the Hebrew (*Shalom aleichem*) and the Arabic (*As-salaam aleikum*), all of which translate literally as "Peace be unto you" and are used as a common greeting.

19 I owe special and particular thanks to my friend, Josh Mansfield, for pointing me in the right direction, which happened to be the Facebook page of the public group Catholic Clerical Dress, Vestments and Vesture by Liturgical Arts Journal, and more specifically to a post by Joshua Clemente on 9 May 2025, identifying the chasuble as the work of the Laboratorio Arte Vesti Sacre, LAVS, based in Rome and Santarcangelo di Romagna. In response to a query from this journalist, press officer Maria Chiara Salvanelli responded for the LAVS, saying the chasuble worn by Pope Leo XIV for the *Missa pro Ecclesia* on 9 May 2025 is the "Celestinian" chasuble made by Filippo Sorcinelli on the occasion of the Celestinian Pardon in L'Aquila on 28 August 2022. The Celestinian Pardon is a special feast day first decreed by Pope St. Celestine V—the last pope to be elected outside a conclave and the last pope outside the Great Western Schism to renounce the papal throne—in 1294. Giuseppe Cardinal Petrocchi gave the chasuble to Pope Francis at the end of the Mass celebrated on the aforementioned occasion in 2022, but Pope Francis never wore it.

20 These days, the suburbicarian sees are Ostia, Albano, Frascati, Palestrina, Porto–Santa Rufina, Sabina–Poggio Mirteto, and Velletri–Segni. Their names have varied slightly through the years, as has their composition. Frascati (the hill town famous for its white wine) is sometimes called Tusculum, after the ancient Roman town nearby, where the Roman statesman and orator, Marcus Tullius Cicero, had a villa (and composed his *Tusculanae disputationes*, a five-book Latin introduction to the great themes

and schools of Greek philosophy). Ostia, the port of Rome, is listed first because it has been for nearly a thousand years—since 1150—the suburbicarian see assigned to the Dean of the College of Cardinals.

21 When the See of Rome is filled, the dean's office functions as sort of unofficial concierge for visiting cardinals. The office is extremely important, however, when the See is vacant. The dean is the principal organizer of the conclave. He also organizes the general congregations ahead of the conclave. Pope Francis introduced a change in 2019, so that the offices of both Dean and vice-Dean of the College of Cardinals would no longer be lifetime appointments. Francis instead made both offices to be filled for five-year mandates, renewable.

The positions of dean and vice-dean are filled by election, with the cardinal bishops getting a vote. As mentioned above, Pope Francis had already expanded the ranks of the cardinal bishops in 2018, ostensibly to foster a wider consultation for the eventual election of a new dean when the time came. Early in 2025, however, Francis decided to forego the election entirely and instead renewed the mandates of the 91-year-old Giovanni Battista Re and the 81-year-old Leonardo Sandri as dean and vice-dean, respectively.

One practical result of that decision was such, that Re and Sandri were responsible for organizing the general congregations and the conclave, while the cardinal secretary of state, Pietro Parolin, 76 years old and a voting cardinal, presided over the conclave inside the Sistine Chapel. See "The dangers of arbitrary government at home and in Rome" by Christopher R. Altieri in *Catholic World Report*, 18 February 2025.

22 The law governing papal elections, Pope St. John Paul II's 1996 *Universi Dominici gregis* (there are also a few supplementary laws enacted by his successors, Pope Francis and Pope Benedict XVI, the pertinent particulars of which we have already discussed), kept the limit of voting-age cardinals as 120, but also kept provisions saying that all cardinals who meet the established requirements and are not otherwise impeded must participate in a conclave, regardless of their total number. Even Pope St. John Paul II frequently created voting cardinals in excess of his own legal limit. Critics of the limit say it is not good to have what is

in essence a rule that has been made to be ignored. On the other hand, the popes have used the limit as a sort of thumb-rule or "ballpark" guide, not so much ignoring it as dancing on either side of it.

23 I told the story in *Reading the News Without Losing Your Faith*, a little volume published with the Catholic Truth Society in 2021:

> I was teaching a class across the river from Vatican Radio headquarters on the day the news broke of Benedict XVI's resignation. The co-ordinator of the English news desk – my dear friend, Charley Collins – knew where I was and knew I had my mobile turned on but set to silent. "In case the Pope dies," I'd told him, "otherwise don't call me while I'm teaching." So, when the phone rang about five minutes into my class and I saw it was Charley calling, I answered right away. He was calling me back to the office urgently because the Pope had just resigned. I didn't quite catch the last word – I was expecting another – and was a little surprised he felt he needed to say why he was calling. "Died?!?" I asked. "Re-signed," said Charley, enunciating carefully. I briefly informed my class that we'd be wrapping up early, explained why, and answered a few questions. Then I ran across the bridge and back to the office, and into a sleepless marathon month of work.

The election of Jorge Mario Cardinal Bergoglio SJ as Pope Francis was thrilling to me, Jesuit-educated as I am (and something of what the Italians call a *gesuita mancato*), somehow despite and somehow because I knew how very challenging it would be to have a son of St. Ignatius Loyola in the See of Peter.

24 The 2019 reform law, *Vos estis lux mundi*, which became a permanent fixture of the Church's body of public law in 2023 after a three-year probationary period and some adjustments, was an imperfect instrument though a marked improvement on the previous framework. See "Challenges for the Catholic Church" by Christopher R. Altieri in *The Wiley Blackwell Companion to Catholicism*, Frederick C. Bauerschmidt, James J. Buckley, Jennifer Newsome Martin, Trent Pomplun, eds., John Wiley & Sons, Ltd., 2024. See also "Responsibility, Accountability, Transparency: The

State of Church Reform" by Christopher R. Altieri in *Catholic Herald*, 24 April 2021.

25 See "Abus sexuels : le cardinal Ricard interdit de ministère public sauf dans son diocese" by Héloïse de Neuville in *La Croix*, 27 September 2023. On the same day the news broke in *La Croix*, the Pontifical Commission for the Protection of Minors issued a blistering "Call to Action" excoriating the Vatican for "tragically harmful deficiencies in the norms intended to punish abusers and hold accountable those whose duty is to address wrong-doing." See also "Pope Francis, Cardinal Ricard, and a stern 'Call to Action'" by Christopher R. Altieri in *Catholic World Report*, 28 September 2023

26 The Zanchetta affair was widely reported, first in the Argentinian press. It broke internationally in early January 2019. The Argentinian prelate and *olim* general secretary of the Argentinian bishops' conference, Gustavo Oscar Zanchetta, knew Pope Francis when the latter was Archbishop of Buenos Aires and president of the conference. Francis made Zanchetta a bishop and put him in the Diocese of Orán, in the far north of Argentina near the border with Bolivia. Francis received allegations of misconduct in 2015, which included compromising images retrieved from Zanchetta's personal cellular phone, but took Zanchetta's word when he protested his phone had been hacked, then returned him to his see. In 2017, after receiving further complaints, Francis let Zanchetta quietly retire "for health reasons" and sent him to a trusty Jesuit for psychological evaluation, after which Francis created a sinecure for Zanchetta inside the Vatican's sovereign asset manager (allegations of irregular asset management against Zanchetta notwithstanding).

A criminal court in Argentina convicted Zanchetta of abusing seminarians and sentenced him to four and a half years imprisonment, most of which he served under house arrest. In June of 2022, Pope Francis sent the canon lawyer who represented Zanchetta to investigate some of the same clerics who had denounced the convicted sex offender to the Vatican and testified against him in the criminal trial. For more, see "Jailed Argentine bishop's lawyer sent by Vatican to investigate priests of his diocese" by Inés San Martín in *Crux*, 24 June 2022. See also "Former Argentine vicar says Vatican knew of bishop's misconduct" by Nicole Winfield and Silvia Noviasky for the Associated Press, 20 January 2019. See also "Interview indicates that Pope Francis knew more than enough about Zanchetta" by Christopher R. Altieri in *Catholic World Report*, 29 May 2019. Veteran Vatican beat reporter Valentina Alazraki of Televisa interviewed Pope Francis and asked him probing questions about the Zanchetta Affair. See "En primicia el Papa en Televisa: 'El mundo sin la mujer no funciona'" on the *Vatican News* website, 28 May 2019. On the broad implications of the case for the Church's clerical and hierarchical leadership culture, see "Zanchetta affair exposes culture of fear, indifference" by Christopher R. Altieri in *Catholic World Report*, 18 March 2019.

27 Pope Francis' remarks about the "altar of hypocrisy" on which he accepted Aupetit's resignation came in response to journalists' queries during an in-flight press conference en route to Rome from Athens on 6 December 2021, roughly two weeks after Aupetit had offered to resign in the face of growing media scrutiny. Aupetit had admitted to an "ambiguous" relationship with a woman in 2012, but insisted the relationship was never sexual. The presumed victim publicly stated she never alleged any possibly criminal misbehaviour. A thorough French police and judicial investigation eventually dismissed the case. Cf. "Soupçons d'agression sexuelle visant Michel Aupetit, ancien archevêque de Paris : enquête classée pour absence d'infraction" AFP wire copy in *Le Monde*, 14 September 2023. Cf. also "Continued errors are costing the Vatican in late innings" by Christopher R. Altieri in *Catholic World Report*, 10 June 2024.

28 This was a niche story, even in the Catholic press, albeit one with broad and powerful implications for the life of the Church as a society with its own laws and customs, and significant import for anyone who would understand the Francis pontificate. The main laws in question vis-à-vis religious life were the 29 June 2016 Apostolic Constitution, *Vultum Dei quaerere*, and its implementing instruction from the Congregation for Institutes of Consecrated Life and Societies of Apostolic Life, *Cor orans*, of 1 April 2018. Pope Francis also enacted several laws—or used other legal instruments—to restrict diocesan bishops' powers to erect religious congregations and even so-called public associations of the faithful, between 2016 and 2022. JD Flynn and Ed Condon,

canon lawyers and the editors of *The Pillar*, co-wrote a helpful rehearsal and analysis of the business in 2022. See "Francis and the power of governance: Understanding the pope's biggest reform" by JD Flynn and Ed Condon in *The Pillar*, 15 June 2022. See also "Synodality vs. Synodality" by Christopher R. Altieri in *The Catholic World Report*, 17 June 2018. See also "As synodality summit looms, navigating a papacy's imperial phase" by John L. Allen Jr. in *Crux*, 26 February 2023.

29 See "Italy wrestles with Pope's annulment reform" by Andrea Gagliarducci for the Catholic News Agency, 13 June 2016.

30 See "The Rule of Law and the Francis Pontificate" by JD Flynn and Ed Condon, in *Catholic World Report*, 25 March 2025.

31 See "Il prelato del lobby gay" by Sandro Magister in *L'Espresso* n. 29, 2013. Cf. Also "Pope Francis and the current crisis of leadership" by Christopher R. Altieri in *Catholic World Report*, 24 September 2018.

32 See "Pope Francis, 1936 – 2025" by Christopher R. Altieri in *Catholic World Report*, 21 April 2025. See also, "The Jesuit Pope and the problematic reform of the Roman Curia" by Christopher R. Altieri in *Catholic World Report*, 15 January 2018.

33 See "How Father Bob Became Pope Leo" by Jason Horowitz, Julie Bosman, et al., in *The New York Times*, 17 May 2025, mentioned herein *passim*.

34 See "Pope Leo XIV: What we know already (and what we can expect)" by Christopher R. Altieri in *Crux*, 11 May 2025. For the remark attributed to Cardinal George, the most recent and frequently cited source is Bishop Robert Barron of Winona-Rochester in Minnesota, a Chicago native who claims George as his mentor. Barron founded his Word on Fire new media apostolate in Chicago, with George's blessing and support.

35 See *Saeculum: History and Society in the Theology of St. Augustine* by R. A. Markus (Cambridge: Cambridge University Press, 1970), especially pp. 25-27. On page 25, Markus notes:

> It is curious that at no time do men seem to have been as ready to speak of an ageing world, or of Rome in her old age, as in the last decades of the fourth century and the early years of the fifth. Neither among Christian nor among pagan Romans was there any sense of a radical transition between

speaking of 'Rome' and of the 'world'. 'Rome' was the head, centre and sum of the 'world'; the 'world' was only the expanded version of the City.

Markus notes, however, that the notion of Rome as having entered upon her old age did not mean Romans—Pagan or Christian—thought of Rome as senile, much less decrepit. "Among pagan writers this did not mean—any more than it meant to Augustine—that the Empire was undergoing senile decay," Markus writes. After the sack of Rome, St. Jerome—a rough contemporary of Saint Augustine—would write: "If Rome can perish, what can be safe? (Ep. 123,16)" It would be Saint Augustine, however, who articulated an understanding of the temporal (saecular) and spiritual spheres, admixed in history, which would not only survive the collapse of Roman power in the West but inform the revival of the whole Western civilizational project. Cf. *Augustine of Hippo* by Peter Brown, esp. pp. 285-296 in the Univ. of California Press edition of 2000 (ch. 25, *Senectus mundi*), and the following two chapters.

36 The Augustinian knows that one of the purposes of law is to preserve a measure of order in societies of men and women who labour under the perduring effects of Original Sin. If one really desires something one ought not—wealth, let us say, beyond reasonably comfortable security—then one's thought will be bent toward the achievement of that object. We cannot hope to solve the problem of avarice by passing laws to make avarice a crime. Humans have tried that. Laws regulate conduct, not thought or desire—at least, not directly—and in any case do not enforce themselves. We have tried reordering society around the idea that ownership itself is criminal, with disastrous result.

37 "Most high, utterly good, utterly powerful, most omnipotent, most merciful and most just," as Saint Augustine puts it in the first book of his *Confessions*, "deeply secret yet most intimately present," even more profoundly secret and at once more intimately present to human nature than anyone is or ever could be, even and especially to oneself. God is secret, not in the sense that He is in Himself abstruse, recondite, or hidden, but in the sense that He is *interior intimo meo et superior summon meo*: "more inward to me than my inmost self and higher than my highest,"

as Saint Augustine famously puts it in Book III.6.xi of his *Confessions*.

38 The encomium, "Echoes with Benedict XVI: 'His dedication to the Church was a blessing for the Augustinians'" is available on the website of the OSA: augustinianorder.org

39 The passage is in Book IX of Augustine's *City of God*, in chapter 20:

> The demons, then, have knowledge without charity, and are thereby so inflated or proud, that they crave those divine honours and religious services which they know to be due to the true God, and still, as far as they can, exact these from all over whom they have influence. Against this pride of the demons, in thrall to which the human race was bound according to its merits, the humility of God had all its great power, which showed itself in Christ; but the souls of men, being inflated with uncleanliness [Lat. *Immunditia*, literally "rubbish"], did not know him, resembling as they did the demons in pride, but not in knowledge.

40 In a lengthy letter to a high Roman official, Flavius Marcellinus, Saint Augustine put the matter as follows:

> Therefore let them, who declare the doctrine of Christ adverse to the republic, give [us] an army of soldiers such as the doctrine of Christ requires them to be; let them give us such provincials, such husbands and wives, such parents and children, such lords, such servants, such kings, such judges— finally, even such debtors and taxpayers and tax-collectors, as Christian doctrine has taught men to be, and then let them dare declare Christian doctrine adverse to the republic; yea, rather, let them no longer hesitate to confess that this doctrine, if it were obeyed, would be the very salvation [*magnam salutem*] of the republic.

Saint Augustine wrote that letter—number 138 in standard collections, it is readily available in translation on the internet— in the year 412 (all years mentioned in this book will be AD, unless otherwise indicated), as he was planning what would become the *City of God*. Letter 138 is essentially a précis of the monumental work in 22 books, written over the span of a decade. Saint Augustine dedicated the first three books of *The City of God* to Marcellinus, his friend and correspondent. Marcellinus, it bears mention, received martyrdom with his brother, Apringius, in 413. The brothers had found themselves in badly with another Roman official who had sympathy for the Donatists—a sort of Christian separatist group with something of a following in North Africa—and were arrested on flimsy charges of collusion with rebels, then executed. The following year, Emperor Honorius officially exonerated Marcellinus.

41 "Humanity," Augustine wrote—he was speaking directly to God—in the opening lines of his *Confessions*, "desires to praise you, insofar as man is part of your creation." By "humanity" Augustine meant human nature, as evidenced by his use of the word, *homo*, Latin for human being as such, male and female. Translating *homo* as "humanity" rather than "man" is a point of style some contemporary readers may find rather consternating, just as others may find it consoling. Sometimes, "humanity" fits. Sometimes, "humanity" does not fit. Consider the next sentence in the passage:

> Man (*homo*), who carries his mortality about with him, the witness of his sin, even the witness that you resist the proud; yet man (*homo*), as part of your creation, desires to praise you.

42 See "Cardinals debating twentieth century problems in a twenty-first century world" by Charles Collins in *Crux*, 2 May 2025.

43 The intervention is available online, thanks to the good offices of veteran Vatican beat journalist Francis X. Rocca, who was working for the Catholic News Service (CNS) of the US bishops in 2012, and also conducted the interview mentioned above. In his intervention, Leo named several Church fathers—great figures of the first several centuries in the Church's history from both East and West—including Saints John Chrysostom (Archbishop of Constantinople, born in Antioch in the mid-fourth century), Ambrose (Bishop of Milan and mentor to Saint Augustine of Hippo), Leo the Great (the fifth-century pope and one of Leo

XIV's namesakes), Gregory of Nyssa (a Cappadocian Father who lived in the fourth century and served two stints as the Bishop of Nyssa in modern-day Türkiye).

44 "Can the Catholic Church Quit the Culture Wars?" by Ross Douthat in *The New York Times*, 24 April 2025.

45 One has to think only of the Zanchetta Affair. V.s., n. 26. It is measurably less likely that a pope conversant with the current technology would accept an explanation like the one Zanchetta offered—his phone had been "hacked"—for the compromising images discovered on it.

46 Leo's remark was more daring than perhaps the casual observer of things Catholic may realize. A statement like that could easily be taken and weaponized by partisans on every side of the so-called "liturgy wars" in the Catholic Church. Traditionalists devoted to the older forms of worship might note how a six-year-old could learn the responses and how being in what was then a boys-only cohort of altar servers certainly fostered his vocation. Those on the other side of the liturgy wars, who are either suspicious of the theological and other ideological commitments one finds particularly among devotees of the old rites, or else who see the "old Mass" and other rites as outdated and even harmful, might detect an indifference to liturgical language and note Leo's emphasis on camaraderie. It was interesting to this observer, that Leo assumed the risk of telling his story as he did, matter-of-fact, acknowledging that history happened, even though history never just happens.

47 Pentecost, i.e., the day on which the very first disciples and believers in the risen Christ received the outpouring of the Holy Spirit. Many of the faithful in the square that day were there as members of the various spiritual movements present in the Church, many of which were born in the wake of the watershed Vatican Council II that ran from 1962–65 and has signed the life of the Church for good and ill through the six decades since it closed.

48 *Cultura dello scarto*, the Italian version of a Spanish expression, *cultura del descarte*, rendered in the Vatican's official English translation of this address as "culture of waste" but more frequently and accurately translated here and elsewhere as "throwaway culture," was a major focus of the Francis pontificate.

49 Theologian Charles Camosy has written with powerfully forceful eloquence on the existential nexus of throwaway cultural phenomena and the deterioration of public space. "There is a deep and growing sense," Camosy wrote in his 2019 book, *Resisting the Throwaway Culture: How a Consistent Life Ethic Can Unite a Fractured People* (Hyde Park, NY; New City Press), "that the whole 'public thing'," i.e., the *res publica*, "is little more than a rigged game." Camosy describes the game as one apparently controlled by a small coterie of unlikelies avid for power (and sometimes just plain avid) and almost perfectly destitute of capacity for humanity in their relations. Somehow and at some point, these people either became or availed themselves of other persons adept at disconnecting—in their own souls and in the world—life's essential operations from justice and the common good. They prefer a set of narrow personal interests (or in the case of the hirelings, a combination of their own and their principals'), and they practise on all of us in pursuit of those narrow interests.

"The polarization and disconnect of our national politics," Camosy went on to say, writing of his own United States of America, "have a symbiotic relationship with the polarization and disconnect within the broader culture." That relationship has produced—is producing—phenomena observable in virtually every culture and society around the globe. Camosy continued:

> In a world dominated by smartphones and social media, many find themselves increasingly disconnected from the physical, the embodied, the real—and especially from authentic encounters with "the other." Given the unprecedented ease of travel and mobility, those with the resources to do so most often choose to live in actual and virtual communities who think pretty much like they do. Whether it is the news we watch, the websites we visit, the people we follow on social media, our physical neighbours, our actual and virtual friends, our churches, or the people with whom we socialize, many of us consume information and engage ideas in ideologically comfortable, largely disconnected communities that rarely force us to examine critically the received wisdom of our ideological community.

Already in 2019, Camosy was describing the phenomenon Collins observed in his 2 May 2025 analysis for *Crux*, in which Collins wrote of how "[t]he algorithms that determine the content users see on social media platforms," algorithms now somehow driving the emerging AI pseudo-persons, "track individuals' posts and 'engagement' with others' posts," i.e., "liking" or otherwise "reacting" to a post or comment, or writing a comment or sharing a meme, and then present users with content the algorithms determine is sufficiently similar to garner more user-engagement. "They show users content the algorithms 'think' the users want to see," Collins wrote, "or else they show them things they think will make users angry – there is some overlap in the categories – basically, anything the algorithm determines likely to garner a click."

50 Pope Francis said:

> Such a mentality can lead to grave violations of the rights of the most vulnerable, to serious injustices and situations of inequality, resulting for the most part from the mindset of profit, efficiency and success. Yet there is also present, in today's throwaway culture, a less visible but extremely insidious factor that erodes the value of the disabled in the eyes of society and in their own eyes. It is the tendency to make individuals view their life as a burden both for themselves and for their loved ones. The spread of this mentality turns the throwaway culture into a culture of death. In the end, "persons are no longer seen as a paramount value to be cared for and respected, especially when they are poor and disabled, 'not yet useful' – like the unborn – or 'no longer needed' – like the elderly" (*Fratelli tutti*, 18). This is so important: the two extremes of life: the unborn with disabilities are aborted, and the elderly close to the end are administered an "easy death," euthanasia, a euthanasia in disguise, but euthanasia all the same.
>
> Combating the throwaway culture calls for promoting the culture of inclusion – the two things go together – by forging and consolidating the bonds of belonging within society. The primary agents of such solidarity are those who, out of a sense of responsibility for the good of each individual, work for greater social justice and for the removal of the barriers

that prevent many people from exercising their basic rights and freedoms. The fruits of these activities are mostly visible in economically more developed countries, where persons with disabilities generally enjoy the right to health care and social assistance, and, even if difficulties are not lacking, are included in many spheres of social life, such as education, culture, the workplace and sports. In poorer countries, this remains, for the most part, a goal to be achieved. Governments that are committed in this regard must thus be encouraged and supported by the international community. It is likewise necessary to support the organizations of civil society, since, without their networks of solidarity, in many places people would be left to themselves.

What is needed, then, is the development of a culture of integral inclusion. The bonds of belonging become even stronger when persons with disabilities are not simply passive receivers, but take an active part in the life of society as agents of change. Subsidiarity and participation are the two pillars of effective inclusion. In this regard, we can appreciate the importance of associations and movements of disabled persons that work to promote their participation in society. (Francis, Address participants in the plenary assembly of the Pontifical Academy for Social Sciences, 11 April 2024)

51 "If you want peace, work for justice." Pope St. Paul VI first used the expression in his Message for the World Day of Peace in 1972.

52 See "Youth's question about the Church not 'Is there space?' but 'Why bother?'" by Christopher R. Altieri in *Crux*, 10 August 2023.

53 The interview, an historic first for Spadaro and *La Civiltà Cattolica*—the flagship Jesuit-run journal of ideas and affairs in Italy, editions of which are vetted by the Secretariat of State of the Holy See—an English version of which ran in *America Magazine*, the Jesuits' leading US publication, as "A Big Heart Open to God: An interview with Pope Francis" by Antonio Spadaro SJ in *America Magazine*, 30 September 2013.

54 See "Curia romana – La riforma di papa Francesco" by Bp. Marcello Semeraro in *Il Regno* n.14/2016, 15 July 2016.

55 The Final Declaration is available online, in English, Spanish, and Portuguese, at propapafrancisco.com

56 See "Antonio Spadaro: «La oposición al Papa no tiene gramática, es polémica e irrespetuosa. Chilla y nada más»" by José Manuel Vidal in *Religión Digital*, 24 November 2017.

57 See "Pope Francis' 'open and incomplete' leadership and the puzzling 'reform' of the Curia" by Christopher R. Altieri in *Catholic World Report*, 19 December 2017.

58 Among the responsibilities of the Congregation for the Doctrine of the Faith (CDF, since 2022 styled the Dicastery for the Doctrine of the Faith or DDF, historically known as the Holy Office of the Inquisition), was vetting papal addresses, homilies, letters, and other documents, as well as documents of other curial departments, for doctrinal clarity and precision. Francis tended to sidestep the CDF, at least for some significant documents issued by his hand or at any rate in his name, a practice that caused at least one protracted spat. The contretemps was over theological imprecisions in Pope Francis' post-Synodal Apostolic Exhortation, *Amoris laetitia*, which broached the possibility of changing the Church's discipline concerning reception of the sacraments by persons in irregular marital and quasi-marital relationships. *Amoris* was susceptible of an orthodox construction, but several bishops (and a few bishops' conferences) enacted special legislation implementing new discipline, occasionally on doctrinally dubious rationale. Observers both within the Vatican and around the Church believed that proper vetting of the document could have accomplished what Francis desired, while avoiding the kerfuffle.

59 "Francis, Trump model 'keep-em-guessing' 21st century leadership" by John L. Allen Jr. in *Crux*, 17 August 2023.

60 See "Pope Francis, Archbishop Fernández, and the question of discipline" by Christopher R. Altieri in *Catholic World Report*, 9 July 2023.

61 Fernández discussed his record, the terms of his appointment to the head office at DDF, and other related issues, in an interview that ran in *The Pillar*. See "'The growth of Catholic theology' – Pope Francis' doctrinal chief speaks" by Edgar Beltrán in *The Pillar*, 17 July 2023.

62 Luis Cardinal Ladaria SJ was head of DDF from 2017, when

Pope Francis declined to renew the five-year mandate of then-Prefect of CDF, the outspoken (and, it turns out, fiscally erratic) Gerhard Cardinal Müller. A native of Majorca and a fellow of unimpeachable orthodoxy, a career academic regarded with high esteem and abiding affection by colleagues and students alike at the Pontifical Gregorian University, Ladaria became secretary at CDF in 2008. It is not lacking in verisimilitude to say Ladaria was as surprised as anyone when Francis tapped him for the top job, the lion's share of the work in which had become the management of disciplinary cases. Ladaria was not trained in forensic work. He was a theoretical thinker, not a criminal investigator. By every account, he had a hard time in the office. For more, see "Pope Francis, Archbishop Fernández, and the question of discipline" by Christopher R. Altieri in *Catholic World Report*, 9 July 2023.

Regarding Müller's erratic fiscal conduct, it is important to note that no impropriety was ever suspected or alleged, even after a more thorough investigation triggered by a spot inspection conducted by the then-recently created Secretariat for the Economy. For more, see "Card. Müller's non-renewal at DDF followed financial investigation" in *The Pillar*, 31 July 2024.

Fr. Robert J. Geisinger SJ, a native of Parma, Ohio, and a member of the order's Midwest Province (formerly Chicago-Detroit), had been in Rome since 2001, serving as the Jesuits' procurator-general (think of the role as chief in-house canonical counsel) to the Jesuit Father General. Pope Francis named him chief prosecutor in 2014. The prosecutor's role had become vacant when then-Promoter of Justice, Msgr. Robert W. Oliver of Boston, was appointed secretary to the Pontifical Commission for the Protection of Minors, which Pope Francis created in 2014 under the leadership of Boston's cardinal archbishop, Sean Patrick O'Malley OFM Cap.

Oliver's unceremonious departure from the PCPM in 2021 was, it happens, a case-in-point illustration of the workaday dysfunction in the Holy See's communications culture. Basically, Oliver discovered not from his superiors but from inquiring journalists, who had called him as he was preparing to board a plane to Boston for what he thought would be a short visit, that his appointment as secretary had not been renewed and that he was without a job in the Vatican. See "American priest reveals communication 'mix-up' about end of Vatican job" by Hannah Brockhaus for the Catholic News Agency, 6 April 2021.

63 See "The Rupnik business will stain and possibly define Pope Francis's legacy" by Christopher R. Altieri in *Catholic World Report*, 24 September 2023. See also "Is Pope Francis protecting Marko Rupnik?" by Robert Mickens in *La Croix International*, 22 September 2023. *La Croix International*, the English-language edition of the French Catholic publication, *La Croix*, is now defunct. *La Croix* announced a strategic reorganization in early 2025, which included a retreat from the North American market. As of summer 2025, *La Croix International*'s website was no longer available, but the article in question has been saved several times by the Internet Archive's Wayback Machine, most recently on 13 December 2024.

64 Responsibility, Accountability, Transparency, i.e., the threefold watchword of Francis' "all-out-battle" against the scourge of abuse and cover-up, declared in 2019 in the wake of several scandals that led Francis to call and organize a four-day safeguarding seminar for senior churchmen at the Vatican. For more, see "Pope Francis's "all-out battle" against clerical abuse has been a failure" by Christopher R. Altieri in *Catholic World Report*, 24 February 2024.

65 See "Cardinal Parolin says he hopes Vatican-China deal can be tweaked" by Andrea Gagliarducci for the Catholic News Agency, 11 April 2022. See also "The Cardinal Zen situation puts spotlight on frayed Vatican-China relations" by Christopher R. Altieri in *Catholic World Report*, 14 May 2022.

66 See "The pope has acknowledged the abuse of nuns but will it make a difference?" by Christopher R. Altieri in *The Catholic Herald*, 14 February 2019. See also, *Women Church World*, February 2020, L. Scaraffia (ed.). See also, "Vatican women's magazine blames drop in nuns on abuses" by Nicole Winfield for the Associated Press, 23 January 2020. See also, "Catholic nun in Africa urges Church to address sexual abuse of women religious" by Ngala Killian Chimtom in *Crux*, 31 May 2025.

67 Kath.net carried the apology in a staff piece, "Kardinal Kasper entschuldigt sich für Afrika-Äußerungen" on 20 October 2014.

68 See "What now for *Fiducia supplicans*?" by Christopher R. Altieri in *Catholic World Report*, 27 December 2023.

69 "Papa Francesco e le coppie gay, spunta il dilemma delle pergamene con la benedizione papale" by Franca Giansoldati in *Il Messaggero*, 30 December 2023.

70 See "*Fiducia supplicans*: Between a rock and a hard place" by Christopher R. Altieri in *Catholic World Report*, 1 January 2024.

71 See "Making History on a Tuesday Morning, With the Church's Blessing" by Amy Harmon Ruth Graham, and Sarah Maslin Nir in *The New York Times*, 19 December 2023

72 See "*Fiducia supplicans* appears to have failed spectacularly" by Christopher R. Altieri in *Catholic World Report*, 23 December 2023.

73 See "Coptic Church cuts theological dialogue with Catholics; says blessing gays 'unacceptable'" by Charles Collins in *Crux*, 9 March 2024.

74 See "A 'bolt out of the blue': Pope Francis sets off an ecumenical earthquake" by Christopher R. Altieri in *Catholic World Report*, 12 May 2023.

75 See "Pope Francis establishes new commission to boost donations to the Holy See" by Justin McClellan for the Catholic News Service in *America Magazine*, 26 February 2025. See also "From hospital, Pope creates commission to aid cash-strapped Vatican" by Elise Ann Allen in *Crux*, 27 February 2025. See also "Pope creates Vatican donations body" by Luke Coppen in *The Pillar*, 26 February 2025.

76 See "Vatican pension deficit estimated at 1.4 billion euros — 10 years ago" staff report in *The Pillar*, 7 April 2025.

77 In any case, a pair of external management and organization consultations, the first by McKinsey & Co.—one of the top three management consultancies in the world, with governments, multinational corporations in major industries, and civil society leaders among their clientele—the second a committee led by Christopher Francis Patten, Baron Patten of Barnes, who had a long and distinguished career in national politics as a Conservative MP before gaining international recognition as the last Governor-General of British Hong Kong, from 1992–7. The Vatican announced the McKinsey communications consultation in December 2013, part of a broader effort to bring Vatican operations up to date and into line with international standards, which also involved the Dutch KPMG tax and advisory group,

Promontory Financial Group, and accounting firm Ernst & Young. The Vatican announced the Patten Committee in July 2014, tasking Patten and ten other members with studying Vatican communications and giving practical advice for the implementation of the McKinsey recommendations.

As Patten explained in a keynote speech at an event sponsored by the Catholic Bishops of England and Wales to mark World Communications Day in 2015, "Our objectives were 'to adapt the Holy See media to changing media consumption trends, enhance coordination and achieve, progressively and sensitively, substantial financial savings'." A linchpin of Patten's reform, in fact, was the creation of a single umbrella office with departments producing content under it for distribution across media and channels. In his 2015 keynote, Patten described the desired arrangement as one in which a "department of content production would create a central content hub overseeing the shared production of general news and media content using the skills and expertise of some of those currently associated primarily with radio, television and print media." The idea was to produce content that was "multi-media in its conception and elaboration" rather than produced by discrete departments or outfits dedicated to one medium, e.g., Vatican Radio for audio stories and *L'Osservatore Romano* for print stories. Patten also envisioned content "available in a range of languages that will be facilitated by the development of a unified translation service which will also service the needs of the Press Office."

Vatican Radio was by far the largest outfit in the Vatican's communications apparatus, and the most expensive. From a purely economic point of view, eliminating redundancies and trimming dead weight were eyes-closed obvious necessities, and urgent. Vatican Radio, because of its size and dedication to what increasingly appeared to be an antiquated medium, was low-hanging fruit. As Patten also made clear in his keynote speech by subtle but unmistakable indications—especially in hindsight, though there were some careful readers knowledgeable of the Vatican communications operation and its culture, who saw even at the time—that the *What?* of the reform had been settled no later than the time of the McKinsey recommendations, and that the business facing the Patten Committee was to answer the *How?* part.

"So, the Vatican Media Committee was established in July 2014, and given a clear mandate to propose reforms," Patten reported in his 2015 keynote. Patten further described himself as "very pleased with the balance that had been found in the membership of the Committee," strongly suggesting but never quite saying it was decided before he agreed to take the head man's role. "It was clear to me that careful thought had gone into the selection of people who were not only professionally qualified as individuals but who, cumulatively, had significant experience in the various dimensions of Church communications and with different media," Patten said. He also said he "particularly liked the mixing of those who were already working within the Vatican structures, of whom there were five, and those who came with a more global experience of the Church and media," of whom there were six, including Patten.

Conspicuously absent from the Committee was Fr. Federico Lombardi SJ, at the time the head of Vatican Radio and the Press Office of the Holy See. The man who had succeeded Lombardi in the directorship of the *Centro Televisivo Vaticano*, Msgr. Dario Viganò, was also absent. Viganò, I mentioned, would become the first Prefect of the Secretariat for Communications of the Holy See—the umbrella organization—created in 2015. Lombardi—a colossal figure who inspired fierce and abiding loyalty from those who served under his leadership—was at once a stalwart defender of Vatican Radio's mission—entrusted to the Jesuits at the outset and carried forward as a work of the Society of Jesus for more than seven decades—who was a devoted son of St Ignatius Loyola and therefore a good soldier, whose time had passed. Dario Viganò was known as a talented—even brilliant—cinematographer and serious student of visual media, especially cinema, whose star was rising but whose time had not quite come.

One way to understand the gathering storm over the communications reform project is as a struggle between the devotees of Old Media and the true believers in the emergent New Media. That would not be wrong—not exactly—and in fact the erstwhile victors in the struggle certainly viewed it that way. From the inside out, however, it appeared rather as a contest between people who saw and those who did not care whether there was or was not a baby in the bathwater. Personnel is policy, as the maxim says, and the persons in charge of the outfit created for the implementation of the communications reform were—if nothing else—the very ones for the job.

The McKinsey report called for massive reductions of overhead, by far the largest contributor to which was salary. Patten's Committee identified redundancies and put forth a plan for consolidation of resources, reduction and combination of roles. It also called—as we have seen—for the creation of a streamlined content production suite. In short, the plan was to cannibalize the old Vatican Radio, slashing and eventually eliminating short-wave transmissions, curtailing AM and FM broadcasts, and shifting focus to digital platforms. Pope Francis wanted the project and the savings it promised, but he did not want to see people let go.

Whether by accident of circumstance or by design, the result was an environment of wariness, especially within the former Vatican Radio, which had been juridically suppressed and folded into the new Secretariat for Communications in early 2016. Hiring freezes were already in place throughout the whole Vatican operation, not only in the communications department. Mandatory retraining and announcements of reductions in both total broadcasts and specific language sections—of which there were more than 40—raised the hackles of the rank-and-file in the former Vatican Radio. "Radio is not television," Collins wrote in his 5 May 2017 analysis for *Crux*, "and neither of them is a newspaper." A single, unified platform may have been able to serve all three, as Collins also noted, and the BBC had succeeded in bringing together text, audio, and video.

Still, it was always going to be a hard sell. Writing a newspaper column and presenting a radio programme simply are not the same thing, and video production is another, entirely. Before and beside the technical objections, there was the sense that journalists were being treated as cogs in a new-fangled public relations machine. "Journalists," Collins wrote, "even for state media, have a role very much different from that of public relations officers." The problem was that the people in charge of the reform gave little indication they knew or cared.

The news that occasioned Collins' considerations was an address by Pope Francis to the participants in the first Plenary Assembly of the Secretariat for Communication, on 4 May 2017. "This Dicastery, which will mark two years on 27 June — two candles — is at the peak of its reform," Francis said. He warned his audience against fear of reform—either the word or the thing—saying that reform is not merely "whitewashing over things" but "giving another form to things," reorganizing. "[I]t must be done intelligently, kindly, Francis went on to say, "but also, also – allow me to use the word – with a bit of 'violence', but good, soft violence, in order to reform things."

"It is in full reform since it is a new reality that is taking steps that are now irreversible," Pope Francis also said. "In this case, in fact, it is not a matter of coordination or a fusion of previous Dicasteries, but of constructing a genuine institution *ex novo*[.]" As Collins astutely noted in his column the next day, *ex novo* is not *ex nihilo*. Some of the reform has come about in the intervening years, though not precisely as envisioned. Anyone who would argue that the communications culture in the Vatican has improved, however, will have a long and rocky road to hoe, while the communications fiascos have been multitudinous and glaring, even scandalous.

78 See "Why it may take 'a little violence' to fix Vatican communications" by Charles Collins in *Crux*, 5 May 2017. For a couple of fairly recent communications cock-ups, see "The Vatican communications fiascos continue" by Christopher R. Altieri in *Catholic World Report*, 5 September 2022. For a major communications debacle from 2009, see "The Lefebvrite case: What was the Vatican thinking?" by John L. Allen Jr. in the *National Catholic Reporter*, 30 January 2009. For an episode from the JPII-era, see "Pope on Gibson movie: Was it as it was?" by John L. Allen Jr., 30 January 2004.

79 See "Vatican media chief resigns over doctored letter scandal" by Nicole Winfield for the Associated Press, 21 March 2018.

80 See "Francis, fake news, and 'snake tactics'" by Christopher R. Altieri in *Catholic World Report*, 25 January 2018.

81 Here is Leo, at length, on the same points:

[T]here is another aspect I would like to recall, complementary

to that of memory, that is the missionary dimension of
the Church and of every institution linked to the Petrine
ministry. This was insisted upon a great deal by Pope Francis
who, consistently with the project laid out in the Apostolic
Exhortation *Evangelii gaudium*, reformed the Roman Curia
from the perspective of evangelization, with the Apostolic
Constitution *Praedicate Evangelium*. And he did this by
following in the footsteps of his predecessors, especially Saint
Paul VI and Saint John Paul II.

As I think you know, the experience of mission forms
part of my life, and not only as a baptized person, as for all
us Christians, but because as an Augustinian religious I was a
missionary in Peru, and in the midst of the Peruvian people
my pastoral vocation matured. I will never be able to thank
the Lord enough for this gift! Then, the call to serve the
Church here in the Roman Curia was a new mission, which
I shared with you during these last two years. And still I
continue it and will continue it, as long as God wills, in this
service that has been entrusted to me.

Therefore, I repeat to you what I said in my first greeting,
in the evening of 8 May: "Together, we must look for ways
to be a missionary Church, a Church that builds bridges and
encourages dialogue, a Church ever open to welcoming…
with open arms, all those who are in need of our charity, our
presence, our readiness to dialogue and our love." These words
were addressed to the Church of Rome. And now I repeat
them, thinking of the mission of this Church towards all the
Churches and the entire world, of serving communion, unity,
in charity and in truth. The Lord gave this task to Peter and
his successors, and you all collaborate in different ways in this
great task. Each one of you gives your contribution, carrying
out your daily work with commitment and also with faith,
because faith and prayer are like salt for food; they impart
flavour.

If, then, we must all cooperate in the great cause of unity
and love, let us seek to do so first of all with our behaviour in
everyday situations, starting also from the work environment.
Each person can be a builder of unity with his attitudes
towards colleagues, overcoming inevitable misunderstandings

with patience, with humility, putting himself in the shoes of others, avoiding prejudices, and also with a good dose of humour, as Pope Francis taught us. (Leo XIV, address to employees of the Holy See and the Vatican City State, 24 May 2025)

82 John L. Allen Jr. of *Crux*, a fellow of Communications and Media at the Word on Fire Institute, published a helpful rehearsal of the business, to which this section is indebted. See "Debunking the Myth of Vast Vatican Wealth" by John. L. Allen Jr. in Word on Fire (at wordonfire.org), 26 September 2024. The Notre Dame and other figures are publicly available.

83 See "Lawsuit charges USCCB misled Catholics about Peter's Pence collection" by Dennis Sadowski for the Catholic News Service, 24 January 2020. The website created by the firm representing plaintiffs, peterspenceclassaction.com, reports the case stalled after the lead attorney, Marc R. Stanley, became US Ambassador to Argentina in 2022.

84 2018 really was *annus horribilis* for the Church. For a brief rehearsal of some of the worst of it, including the matters mentioned above, see "2018: The year the Church's crisis was unmasked" by Christopher R. Altieri in *Catholic World Report*, 31 December 2018.

85 For an excellent précis of the situation, see "How the Vatican manages money and where Pope Leo XIV might find more" by Nicole Winfield for the Associated Press, 7 June 2025.

86 For the Guerrero interview, see "Fr. Guerrero: Peter's Pence supports the mission of the Church" by Andrea Tornielli for *Vatican News*, 25 June 2021.

87 For a very detailed recent breakdown of spending patterns and a thorough analysis of the data available, see "Who's Spending Peter's Pence?" by Brendan Hodge in *The Pillar*, 11 July 2025.

88 For the law making APSA the responsible organ for real and moveable assets of the Holy See, see *Praedicate Evangelium* 219, §1-2. For the August 2022 rescript, see "Pope: All movable assets of Holy See to be managed by IOR" staff report in *Vatican News*, 23 August 2022.

89 See "Why Pope Francis' Vatican bank order is a big deal" by Ed Condon in *The Pillar*, 23 August 2022.

90 See "Workers (again, and again) beg the Vatican to face its personnel problem" by John L. Allen Jr. in *Crux*, 14 July 2024.

91 See "A breezy (and cautionary) history of the papal 'dark age'" by Christopher R. Altieri in *Catholic World Report*, 22 November 2021.

92 In the heyday of the papal states, the papacy could support itself on the backs of the taxpaying tradesmen, landowners, and merchant classes, with other income from the faithful throughout Europe. After the French Revolution and the post-Napoleonic settlement—which saw the Church beset on all sides—the papal states fell into irreversible decline and eventually collapsed. It was Bl. Pius IX who revived Peter's Pence in the dark years following the papal states' collapse. It was Pope Leo XIV's most recent namesake-predecessor, Pope Leo XIII, who got the Holy See involved in (mostly Roman and Italian) real estate.

The Banco Ambrosiano scandals of the late 1970s and early 1980s put the Holy See in a terrible financial bind—indeed, very nearly bankrupted the Holy See—and that was with an archbishop from the United States, Paul Marcinkus, in the leadership of the IOR. The Banco Ambrosiano, it bears mention, was founded in 1896, specifically and explicitly with a Catholic mission as a sort of prototypical "ethical investor" nearly a century before the term gained currency. For several decades starting in the rough middle of the twentieth century, the Banco Ambrosiano began to expand its operations. By the time Roberto Calvi became chairman, the bank was poised as a significant international financial operator. During Calvi's tenure in the leadership of the bank, several senior bank officials were embroiled in mafia scandals. In the early 1980s, Italian authorities uncovered what they believed were connections to an Italian Masonic lodge, *Propaganda Due* (P2), and Calvi himself was convicted of criminal financial misconduct. Calvi appealed the conviction and was released pending appeal, but his body was found hanging beneath Blackfriars Bridge in London in the late spring of 1982.

One of the more significant efforts Pope St. John Paul II made in the wake of the Banco Ambrosiano scandal was the creation of the Papal Foundation, a stewardship fund at the service of the Holy See, which makes grants for specific charitable projects.

The Papal Foundation was the subject of scandal in 2019, when US cardinals faced a donor uprising over what they perceived to be strong-arm tactics from the Vatican and Pope Francis, led by then-Cardinal Theodore McCarrick. The Papal Foundation has since reorganized under strengthened lay leadership.

93 It occurs to me that I used a version of this analogy to articulate one of the great challenges facing the cardinal electors as they went into conclave. See "Challenges facing the conclave" by Christopher R. Altieri in *Catholic World Report*, 30 April 2025.

94 On the breaking of the Rupnik business, with early reportage of the CDF decision to rule the charges statute-barred, see "Jesuit artist has ministry cut; Vatican doesn't prosecute" by Nicole Winfield for the Associated Press, 6 December 2022. See also, "Jesuit priests demand transparency in Vatican's artist case" by Nicole Winfield for the Associated Press, 7 December 2022. See also, "The Fr. Rupnik case: What is wrong with these people?" by Christopher R. Altieri in *Catholic World Report*, 22 December 2022.

95 For the expulsion, see "In l'Affaire Rupnik, optics matter (too)" by Christopher R. Altieri in *Catholic World Report*, 16 June 2023. For the news Rupnik had sought release from his Jesuit vows before he was expelled, for the claims of then-Director of Rupnik's Centro Aletti, Maria Campatelli, and for Rupnik's supposed radioactivity, see "Rupnik Affair exposes leadership crisis in Jesuits, Roman Curia" by Christopher R. Altieri in *Catholic World Report*, 18 June 2023, and "The Rupnik affair is casting a long and growing shadow" by Christopher R. Altieri in *Catholic World Report*, 24 July 2023.

96 See "Fr Marko Rupnik incardinated in Slovenian diocese" by Luke Coppen in *The Pillar*, 25 October 2023.

97 See "The Rupnik affair goes from scandalous to contemptible" by Christopher R. Altieri in *Catholic World Report*, 25 October 2023.

98 A complete rehearsal of the Rupnik Affair would run to great length. Indeed, the subject deserves the fullest possible treatment, though anything approaching even adequate discussion would be far beyond the scope of this book. The following summary statement of the next major events in it, however, will be bad enough. Briefly, then: It emerged that Vatican investigators

had determined—in January of 2022, nearly a year before the Rupnik Affair began to come before the public—that there was a case for Rupnik to answer. In October of 2022, however, the Congregation for the Doctrine of the Faith (CDF, i.e., the Vatican department responsible for handling cases like the one against Rupnik, later styled the Dicastery for the Doctrine of the Faith or DDF) had decided not to prosecute him, citing an expired statute of limitations.

Italian blogs were the first to report whispers of bad doing around Rupnik, which the Associated Press and eventually others picked up and began to investigate. In short order, it further emerged that Rupnik had been secretly tried in 2019 and secretly convicted of a serious canonical crime in 2020, then secretly punished for his crime—with excommunication, a "medicinal" punishment meant to obtain some expression of remorse and to be lifted as soon as such expression is forthcoming, which Rupnik gave, after which the secret punishment was secretly lifted—fully two years before the serial abuse allegations came to light. (The crime of which a secret canonical tribunal had secretly convicted Rupnik in 2020 was one of the most serious contemplated under Church law: "Absolution of an accomplice in a sin against the Sixth Commandment of the Decalogue"; in essence, when a priest or bishop hears the confession of a person with whom the cleric had engaged in illicit sexual relations. At that point, the first of several major unanswered questions in the affair began to take shape. It remains unclear why the Congregation for the Doctrine of the Faith refused to waive the statute of limitations and allow Rupnik to face justice.

Statutes of limitations exist primarily to guarantee the integrity of judicial process, particularly to guarantee that the accused party has the wherewithal to mount a worthy defence. In Rupnik's case, the accused was in good health and his accusers were available for confrontation. Investigators had compiled mountainous other evidence equally available to defence counsel for examination. Then, there was the fact of the secret trial, which had ended in a guilty verdict and punishment. There was, in short, no apparent good reason not to lift the statute bar, nor has anyone in a position to give any such explanation ever proffered one.

Later in December of 2022, one of Rupnik's alleged victims, Gloria Branciani, described the abuse she suffered to the Italian news magazine, *Domani*. The English-language digital investigative news project, *The Pillar*, reproduced the entire piece in translation. "Father Marko [Rupnik] asked me to have threesomes with another sister of the community," Branciani recounted:

> [B]ecause sexuality had to be, in his opinion, free from possession, in the image of the Trinity where, he said, "the third person would welcome the relationship between the two." On those occasions, he would ask me to live out my femininity in an aggressive and dominant way, and since I could not do so, he would deeply humiliate me with phrases that I cannot repeat.

"Father Marko at first slowly and gently infiltrated my psychological and spiritual world," Branciani told *Domani* in that December 2022 interview, "by appealing to my uncertainties and frailties while using my relationship with God to push me to have sexual experiences with him." Branciani described how Rupnik pressed "for more and more erotic games in his studio at the Collegio del Gesù in Rome," a residence for Jesuits studying at the Pontifical Gregorian University (founded in 1551 by St. Ignatius Loyola himself, as the *Collegium Romanum*, the oldest and most prestigious Jesuit university on the face of the Earth, and this journalist's *alma mater*), which stands adjacent the Jesuit mother church—the Church of the Gesù—in Rome. Branciani said Rupnik would practise his depravities "while painting or after the celebration of the Eucharist or confession." Subsequent reporting further attested to Rupnik's habitual use of his "creative process" as part of his grooming and abuse, making his artwork inseparable from his depravity and therefore unsuitable for the adornment of sacred space.

It bears mention, as well, that Rupnik's erstwhile Jesuit superiors both in the priest's native Slovenia and in Rome had heard tell of his behaviour more than a decade before any of the foregoing came before the public. Not only did they never take meaningful action against him. They either turned a blind eye toward efforts to discredit and besmirch the names of Rupnik's accusers, or else actively participated in efforts to make sure he would never face significant consequences for his actions. Some of the names of those Jesuits allegedly involved in the Rupnik business were prominent figures in the Society of Jesus.

Fr. Francisco Egaña SJ, who was vice-rector of the Pontifical Gregorian University when this journalist was a graduate student there, held several important positions in the Jesuits' senior leadership structure for more than two decades. Egaña, who died 30 June 2019, allegedly heard of Fr. Rupnik's behaviour no later than 1998, from Mirjam Kovač. Egana, however, was not the first Jesuit in Rome to hear allegations. Tomáš Josef Card. Špidlík SJ, a highly regarded professor of spirituality at the Gregorian and a noted figure in the Czech language programme of the Jesuit-run Vatican Radio since the dark days of the Cold War and Communist oppression in Eastern Europe, heard from Branciani of her troubles in 1993.

"In August 1993," Branciani told *Our Sunday Visitor*, "[then-Father] Špidlík advised me to write a letter of resignation." Branciani also told OSV how Špidlík "suggested saying there were no precise reasons for my request for dispensation from [her religious] vows." Špidlík, who died in 2010, was Rupnik's close friend and a board member of the Centro Aletti art centre in Rome, of which Rupnik was the founding director and at which he came to reside permanently in 1993, after Archbishop Alojzij Šuštar of Ljubljana—who had heard tell of Rupnik's misdeeds from Branciani as well—quietly removed Rupnik from the Loyola Community of Mengeš in north-central Slovenia (then under Šuštar's jurisdiction), a house of religious sisters belonging to the congregation Rupnik had helped to establish in the 1980s in his native Slovenia, and advised for several years. Pope St. John Paul II gave Špidlík the red hat in 2003. (See "'No one listened,' says alleged Rupnik victim, recalling fight with church system for truth" by Federica Tourn in *Our Sunday Visitor*, 30 November 2023.)

It would be more than a decade and a half—some 16 years—before formal accusations against Rupnik would finally make their way to authorities in the Vatican. It would be by way of another Jesuit, Bishop Daniele Libanori SJ, an auxiliary of

Rome sent by Pope Francis to investigate claims of misrule in the Loyola Community under Sr. Ivanka Hosta, foundress of the Community with Rupnik.

Another Jesuit—Luis Card. Ladaria SJ—was prefect of the Congregation for the Doctrine of the Faith at the time, and another Jesuit—Fr. Robert Geisinger SJ—was chief prosecutor (styled—not without some bitter irony—"Promoter of Justice" in ecclesiastical nomenclature). The Associated Press obtained some of Libanori's correspondence, in which the Jesuit bishop-investigator said the allegations against Rupnik were correct. Rupnik's victims, Libanori wrote, had "seen their lives ruined by the evil suffered and by the [Church's] complicit silence." (See "Vatican investigator says claims of Jesuit abuse true" by Nicole Winfield for the Associated Press, 19 December 2022.)

The Jesuits expelled Rupnik for disobedience but did not seek his dismissal from the clerical state, and Rupnik received an invitation from Bishop Jurij Bizjak of Koper, to serve as a priest of that diocese in Rupnik's native Slovenia. When that news reached the public, as it did on 25 October 2023, it triggered incandescent worldwide outrage and sustained global outcry. (See "How the Jesuits could have laicized Rupnik, and why they should have" by Ed Condon in *The Pillar*, 25 July 2023. See also "Fr Marko Rupnik incardinated in Slovenian diocese" by Luke Coppen in *The Pillar*, 25 October 2023.)

Two days later, on 27 October 2023, a statement from the press office of the Holy See announced that Pope Francis had decided to waive the statute of limitations and order a review of the Rupnik case. "In September," the statement from the Vatican press office read, "the Pontifical Commission for the Protection of Minors brought to the Pope's attention that there were serious problems in the handling of the Fr. Marko Rupnik case and lack of outreach to victims." On its own, that claim was not perfectly lacking in verisimilitude. The founding president of the Pontifical Commission for the Protection of Minors, Sean Patrick O'Malley OFM Cap (then the Archbishop of Boston), had shown himself willing to speak frankly and directly in criticism of Francis' failures in leadership on abuse, cover-up, and outreach to victims. As an institution, however, the Pontifical Commission for the Protection of Minors had long since acquired a reputation for dysfunction and had been criticized by both observers and members—among them three founding members who resigned at different times, all in frustration—as ineffectual within the Vatican system. (See "Waiving the statute of limitations makes matters worse in Rupnik affair" by Christopher R. Altieri in *Catholic World Report*, 25 October 2023. See also "Justice in Rupnik case must be thorough, public, completely transparent" by Christopher R. Altieri in *Catholic World Report*, 28 October 2023.)

Francis had created the Commission as an autonomous body outside the Roman Curia early in his pontificate—on 22 March 2014—and then folded the Commission into the curial system on 19 March 2022, when he promulgated his Apostolic Constitution, *Praedicate Evangelium*, reforming the offices and general structure of the Roman Curia. The PCPM, as it had come to be known, had earned its reputation despite—or perhaps because of—O'Malley's willingness to criticize Francis publicly. Documents reviewed by this journalist at the time showed the Commission sending overtures to Rupnik's victims on 8 October of 2023, giving the powerful impression that the PCPM was still beginning to gather information in the middle of October, weeks after Francis should have received the aforesaid warnings from the PCPM of irregularities in the management of the Rupnik case. It is also noteworthy that, in the meantime, the PCPM had taken to styling itself in correspondence as the Pontifical Commission for the Protection of Minors and Vulnerable Persons, though it had at the time neither official designation nor statutory authority to concern itself with vulnerable persons who were not minors. In any case, it simply beggars credulity to claim (or even suggest) that Pope Francis only learned of problems with the handling of the Rupnik business in September of 2023. The Rupnik case had been before the public for the better part of a year. (See "Waiving the statute of limitations makes matters worse in Rupnik affair" by Christopher R. Altieri in *Catholic World Report*, 25 October 2023. On the PCPM, O'Malley, and Francis, see "Pope Francis, Cardinal Ricard, and a stern 'Call to Action' by Christopher R. Altieri in *Catholic World Report*, 28 September 2023. O'Malley's statement is available on the PCPM website, tutelaminorum.org under "Cardinal O'Malley Urges Pastoral Prudence" dated 28 June 2024.)

More to the point, the Rome vicariate—the governing and administrative apparatus of the Rome diocese—under Rome's cardinal vicar, Angelo De Donatis, had issued a statement on 19 September 2023 (a Tuesday) announcing that the vicariate had conducted its own internal investigation of Rupnik's Centro Aletti art centre and given the centre a clean bill of health. The statement said De Donatis had personally ordered a canonical visitation of the Centro Aletti on 16 January 2023, claiming canonical authority over the centre in virtue of its having been erected as a "public association of the faithful" of the Rome diocese in 2019 (after its founding in the early 1990s as a work of the Society of Jesus attached to the Pontifical Oriental Institute) and appointing Msgr. Giacomo Incitti, as investigator (officially styled a Visitor). Incitti, a diocesan priest of Frosinone (officially the Diocese of Frosinone-Veroli-Ferentino, which is immediately exempt to the Holy See, meaning it is not part of an ecclesiastical province, not even the province of Rome) and law professor at Rome's Pontifical Urbaniana University, apparently had a broad mandate from De Donatis. The statement from the Rome vicariate said Incitti had discovered 'gravely anomalous procedures' surrounding Rupnik's aforementioned secret 2020 excommunication for criminal absolution of an 'accomplice' in a 'sin against the Sixth Commandment'. That finding immediately raised questions—at present also unresolved—concerning how and why a canonical visitation of Rupnik's art centre should have been so broad in scope as to warrant the investigator access to secret CDF trial records. (On De Donatis' statement and the "visitation" that occasioned it, see "Will anyone in Rome get to the bottom of the Rupnik/Centro Aletti business?" by Christopher R. Altieri in *Catholic World Report*, 19 September 2023.)

On 15 September 2023—a Friday, it happened, a mere four days before the Rome vicariate issued its note regarding the investigation of the Centro Aletti ordered by De Donatis—Maria Campatelli, Rupnik's longtime associate and the director of the Centro Aletti at the time, had a private audience with Pope Francis. Campatelli had already made waves in June of

2023, as spring was about to turn into summer, when she issued a statement through the Centro Aletti (dated 17 June 2023) revealing that Rupnik had in fact requested release from the Society of Jesus several months before the Jesuits dismissed him—something the Society of Jesus had failed to mention in their own public communications regarding the Rupnik affair and their part in it—and that several other Jesuits attached to the Centro Aletti were also seeking release from the Society, having 'lost confidence in the leadership of their Jesuit superiors'. In her June statement, Campatelli had also called the accusations against Rupnik 'unproven and defamatory' though she did not claim—not in words—that they were false. (For Campatelli's private audience with Pope Francis, see "Pope Francis meets close collaborator of Rupnik" by Hannah Brockhaus for the Catholic News Agency, 15 September 2023. For Campatelli's June statement, see "Rupnik Affair exposes leadership crisis in Jesuits, Roman Curia" by Christopher R. Altieri in *Catholic World Report*, 18 June 2023.)

News of Pope Francis' decision to lift the statute bar was stunning, in short, but not reassuring. The decision appeared to be a reversal. At any rate, Francis had not lifted the statute bar before October of 2023, despite already colossal and ever-growing evidence of grave crime and serious mismanagement (at very least) at every level, as well as intense public scrutiny and increasing impatience. It was also a decision that further complicated Francis' already problematic execution of his own stated policies and policy rationale regarding statutes of limitations.

"With the abused vulnerable adult," Pope Francis had told the AP in an interview published in January of that same year, "it is the same as if the victim were a minor, practically," and, "I do not tolerate the statute of limitations when there is a minor involved." In such cases, Francis said, "Of course, I lift it right away." That answer raised two further questions, the first being why he had not lifted the statute bar in Rupnik's case. That question shaded perceptibly into the second, which regarded the definition of "vulnerable adult" as a legal category, a question never clearly answered either in statute or in jurisprudence. (See "Pope opens up on sex abuse cases, says church must do more" by Nicole Winfield for the Associated Press, 25 January 2023.)

In that January 2023 interview with the AP, Pope Francis had also said he did not intervene in the case against Rupnik when it was first before the CDF in 2021, but then said that he had something to do with "a small procedural thing" pertaining to the case. The statement was troubling, perplexing, revealing. One may have nothing to do with the management of a case, or one may have something to do with the management of a case. One may not simultaneously have nothing to do with a case and something to do with that same case, however great or small the something may be. (See also, "Pope Francis's remarks to AP about Rupnik are confusing and contradictory" by Christopher R. Altieri in *Catholic World Report*, 28 January 2023.)

Pope Francis, whether he had nothing to do directly with the management of the Rupnik case or something to do directly with the management of the Rupnik case, had everything to do with the management of the Rupnik case. Francis always had power to order the lifting of the statute bar, for example, so "nothing" was all Francis had to do in order to see that Rupnik never face ecclesiastical justice for his crimes. Quite apart from direct decisions or non-decisions in the management of the Rupnik case, Francis gave powerful indication of support for Rupnik, when Francis used a mosaic depiction of the Madonna and Child by Rupnik as a prop in a recorded video message to participants in a Marian Congress in Aparecida, Brazil. That was in June of 2023, more than six months after the details of the Rupnik case had begun to come before the public. It also gave cover to Ruffini and the Dicastery for Communication, which continued to use digital images of Rupnik works. (See "Head of Vatican communications strongly defends continued use of Rupnik art" by Christopher R. Altieri in *Catholic World Report*, 22 June 2024. See also, "He who keeps silent is to be taken as consenting…" by Christopher R. Altieri in *Catholic World Report*, 25 June 2024.)

99 See "Rupnik case complex, but in 'advanced stage,' Vatican official says" by Elise Ann Allen in *Crux*, 30 May 2024.

100 The precise figure for Montana's judicial branch is $60,595,286 and for the Department of Justice was $150,184,775. The figures are available on the budget.mt.gov website. The 2020 US census

put Montana's population at 1,084,225. Tax rate information comes from the nonprofit Tax Foundation and Montana.gov

101 See "Pope Francis's 'all-out battle' against clerical abuse has been a failure" by Christopher R. Altieri in *Catholic World Report*, 24 February 2024.

102 Charles Collins has written extensively about the reserve powers doctrine for several years. In a 2021 article special to the *Catholic Herald*, Collins wrote:

> UK monarchs [know] better than to test their power. This is why most of the monarch's theoretical powers are either exercised through her Ministers, or not exercised at all. Such discretion helped keep the British monarchy popular, and keeps Parliament from chipping away what remains of the royal power in theory.
>
> There is no reason for such a principle not to be established at the Vatican, no reason for legislation not to pass without loopholes, no reason for the pontiff's fingers not to be kept off the levers of justice, including the penalty phase.
>
> The papal prerogative, like the royal prerogative, would be held in reserve[.]

For more, see "Huzzah! Or, what a bawdy historical drama can teach us about Church reform" by Charles Collins in *The Catholic Herald*, 3 March 2021.

103 Any reader who has noticed that the dogmatic definition of the papal supremacy came not from a pope but an ecumenical council, may also have wondered how that very fact does not on its own unsettle the settlement. The answer, in short, is that dogmatic definitions are irreformable. Once a dogmatic definition is given—whether by a pope acting alone and on his own authority or by an ecumenical council (which, it turns out, cannot issue decrees without papal assent)—no power may repeal or even revise or otherwise alter it. Not even a later pope or another ecumenical council, nor even the same pope or ecumenical council, may later alter it.

On a real, practical, nuts-and-bolts level, therefore, the Fathers of the Vatican Ecumenical Council I bound themselves and their successors, as well as the pope and all future popes, to their definition of the papal supremacy, which—it bears repeating—also asserted the rights of other bishops and the faithful. The Dogmatic Constitution, *Pastor Aeternus*, with which the Vatican Council I dogmatically defined the papal supremacy, also took pains to articulate the scope of the supremacy:

> This power of the Supreme Pontiff by no means detracts from that ordinary and immediate power of episcopal jurisdiction, by which bishops, who have succeeded to the place of the apostles by appointment of the Holy Spirit, tend and govern individually the particular flocks which have been assigned to them. On the contrary, this power of theirs is asserted, supported and defended by the Supreme and Universal Pastor; for St. Gregory the Great says: "My honour is the honour of the whole Church. My honour is the steadfast strength of my brethren. Then do I receive true honour, when it is denied to none of those to whom honour is due."

If the Vatican Council I's dogmatic definition of papal supremacy settled the conciliarist question on the macro level—and that is a very big *If*— but grant it for the moment and for the sake of argument—that same settlement also opened a veritable Pandora's Box of problems for ecclesiastical justice on the micro level and indeed at every level in between.

104 Hamilton's "Opinion on the Constitutionality of Establishing a National Bank" was one of two opinions solicited by the President of the United States, George Washington. The other, taking a view very much contrary to Hamilton's, came from Thomas Jefferson, who served as Washington's Secretary of State. Hamilton was Washington's Secretary of the Treasury. Both papers are included in all the standard collections and are widely available online.

105 The case of Archbishop Anthony Apuron of Agaña, encompassing the US territorial island of Guam in the Pacific, may serve to illustrate the point. Apuron was accused of criminal sexual misconduct with a minor and of criminal financial misconduct. The local papers covered the story thoroughly and the Catholic press followed when the case reached Rome, which it eventually did, though not without twists and turns

too numerous and complicated to rehearse here. Suffice it to say that Apuron abused minors—he has always denied the charges, despite a guilty verdict in canonical court—and was alleged to have abused his office in attempts to interfere with the Church's own oversight and investigative mechanisms.

The Vatican announced in 2016 that the prefect emeritus of the Apostolic Signatura (the Catholic Church's highest ordinary tribunal), Raymond Leo Cardinal Burke, would preside over the panel of judges appointed to gather evidence and try a case against Apuron. A senior churchman with particular devotion to the Traditional Latin Mass and other older liturgical rituals, as well as avowed sympathies for and connection with "traditionalist" communities in communion with the whole Church, Burke had been an occasionally outspoken critic of Pope Francis. Burke's appointment perhaps indicated Francis' confidence in the cardinal's canonical acumen and willingness to trust him with an important and sensitive matter. It was nevertheless recklessly and inaccurately spun in some traditionalist circles as a case of Francis dispatching Burke to a small island in the Pacific in order to get him out of Rome.

In any case, Burke was given the conduct of the trial, but no formal charges were ever published, the notoriety of the case notwithstanding. Apuron's trial at first instance concluded in a guilty verdict. The press office of the Holy See carried a statement from the Apostolic Tribunal of the Congregation for the Doctrine of the Faith, under whose auspices Burke et al. had conducted the trial, which acknowledged that "abuse of minors" were among the charges Apuron had faced, and reported that the archbishop had been found "guilty of certain of the accusations" but failed to specify which or to say whether he had been acquitted of others. In full, the statement read:

> The canonical trial in the matter of accusations, including accusations of sexual abuse of minors, brought against the Most Reverend Anthony Sablan APURON, O.F.M.Cap., Archbishop of Agaña, Guam, has been concluded.
>
> The Apostolic Tribunal of the Congregation for the Doctrine of the Faith, composed of five judges, has issued its sentence of first instance, finding the accused guilty of

certain of the accusations and imposing upon the accused the penalties of privation of office and prohibition of residence in the Archdiocese of Guam.

The sentence remains subject to possible appeal. In the absence of an appeal, the sentence becomes final and effective. In the case of an appeal, the imposed penalties are suspended until final resolution.

While Franz Kafka may not have approved fully of the statement, it is nonetheless unlikely to stand as a model of clarity in communication. In the event, Apuron did appeal. His appeal was rejected and his sentence confirmed. The Vatican statement announcing the failure of Apuron's appeal was the first official confirmation that Apuron had in fact been found guilty of canonical sex crimes against minors.

Pope Francis discussed the Apuron case during an in-flight press conference on 26 August 2018—after the guilty verdict and while the appeal was pending—adding another wrinkle to an already polyptych case. "I decided," Francis said, "because [Apuron's] is a very difficult case, to take the privilege that I have of taking on the appeal myself and not sending it to the council of appeal that does its work with all the priests." Francis was not a trained canonist, however, a fact that raised the question—not for the first time or the last in his pontificate—why he would arrogate direct responsibility to himself. Francis went on to how he "made a commission of canonists" to assist him, and that they had promised a recommendation "after a maximum of a month" following Francis' return from Dublin, so that Francis could "make a judgment."

The statement from the Vatican press office announcing the failure of Apuron's appeal and the confirmation of his sentence, however, reported as follows:

As was announced on 16 March 2018, the Apostolic Tribunal of the Congregation for the Doctrine of the Faith concluded a First Instance canonical penal trial in the case of the Most Reverend Anthony Sablan Apuron, O.F.M.Cap. (Agaña, Guam). As was noted at the time, an appeal was possible and was in fact lodged. That appeal has been concluded. On 7

February 2019, the Tribunal of Second Instance upheld the sentence of First Instance finding the Archbishop guilty of delicts against the Sixth Commandment with minors. The penalties imposed are as follows: the privation of office; the perpetual prohibition from dwelling, even temporarily, in the jurisdiction of the Archdiocese of Agaña; and the perpetual prohibition from using the insignia attached to the rank of Bishop. This decision represents the definitive conclusion in this case. No further appeals are possible.

While technically accurate in any case, the statement did not make clear who constituted the appellate court. It could have been Pope Francis, himself. It could have been the ordinary appellate tribunal.

During that same 2018 in-flight presser en route to Rome from Dublin, Pope Francis also made reference to another reform law he decreed to much fanfare in 2014: *Come una madre amorevole*—"As a loving mother"—which gave the pope the structural juridical wherewithal to remove negligent bishops without trial. Bishops often gravely miscarried in their duty without, however, committing any crime at either canon or civil law, especially in respect of abuse. The utility of a legal framework providing for the relatively easy removal of gravely and/or habitually negligent prelates even and especially when their negligence is not manifestly criminal, was apparent. Francis told journalists, however:

> [*As a loving mother*] was subsequently seen neither to be feasible nor suitable for the different cultures of the bishops who should be judged. We are taking the recommendation of *As a loving mother* and setting up a jury for each bishop, but that is not the same thing. A particular bishop has to be judged and so the pope sets up a jury [i.e., a panel of judges] more capable of taking that case. It is something that works better, also because, for a group of bishops to leave their dioceses... [*sic*] for this reason it is not possible. So, the tribunals and the [panels of judges] change.
>
> This is the way we have done things up to now. A number of bishops have been judged this way: the latest was the

archbishop of Guam, who appealed his sentence, and I decided—because it was a very, very complex case—to make use of the right that I have, hear his appeal on my own, and not to send him to the appeal court that carries out its work with priests. I took it up personally. I set up a commission of canon lawyers to help me, and they told me that, in a short time, a month at most, they would offer a "recommendation" so that I could make a judgement. It is a complicated case on the one hand, but not difficult, because the evidence is extremely clear; from the standpoint of evidence, it is clear.

Why Francis would take the adjudication of a difficult case upon himself, even though he has neither training nor experience as a canonist, is a question that has never received adequate answer. Why the Apuron case—one in which the bishop was accused of abuse—should have proved anything about the viability of a law introduced to deal with negligent prelates, was likewise unclear. In any case, it should have been news— major news—when Francis said that several bishops had been subjected to some sort of judicial or para-judicial process for negligence or worse.

Francis, however, dropped that piece of otherwise very newsworthy information on the same day a much bigger scandal broke: Archbishop Carlo Maria Viganò's spectacular *J'accuse!* alleging, among other things, systematic cover-up of the disordered and criminally abusive behaviour of the former Archbishop of Washington, Theodore Edgar "Uncle Ted" McCarrick. A career official in the Secretariat of State and former nuncio to the United States, Carlo Maria Viganò is a sad case and a cautionary tale, whose allegations nevertheless deserved careful vetting. His initial allegations, detailed in an 11-page letter, unsurprisingly and justifiably triggered a media fracas. So, Francis' description of his own law as "unfeasible" and in any case a mere "recommendation" went largely unnoticed. Francis' cryptic mention of bishops more-or-less secretly tried in specially created courts also flew mostly under the radar. A complete account of bishops who have faced judgment remains to this day outstanding.

In such an environment, with such a recent history, it will be difficult for Pope Leo XIV and his people to convince either the

faithful or the broad public of their earnest regarding the responsibility, accountability, and most of all transparency.

106   See "How Pope Francis could get back into the game on sex
abuse reform" by Charles Collins in *Crux*, 25 July 2018.

107   See "Is a Catholic 'Victims' Rights' movement the next frontier
in abuse reform?" by John L. Allen Jr. in *Crux*, 22 December
2019. See also "Vatican tells bishops to get serious on crime and
punishment" by Elise Ann Allen in *Crux*, 1 June 2021.

108   Pope Francis garnered significant good press for a change he made
in 2019, to the use of the so-called "pontifical secret"—roughly,
the top-secret classification within the Holy See's system—in
cases of abuse and cover-up. In reality, Francis' modification only
changed the default level of secrecy from the highest to the
"normal" level of secrecy. The difference, in short, was that everything related to criminal investigations and trials went from being
under pontifical secret unless specifically and explicitly removed,
to a state of affairs in which investigations and trials on sex crimes
charges are not under pontifical secret unless they are specifically
and explicitly placed under it. For more, see "The change to the
'pontifical secret' does less than it appears to do" by Christopher
R. Altieri in *The Catholic Herald*, 18 December 2019.

109   See "Vatican court hands down first-ever conviction for sexual
abuse" by Elise Ann Allen in *Crux*, 25 January 2024.

110   In the England of the late fifteenth century, King Henry VII
established the Court of Star Chamber for the trial—in secret—
of persons either too powerful or too highly regarded for fair
trial in open court. It was not long before the powerful and well-
connected discovered ways to use Star Chamber against their
enemies both political and personal. "Star Chamber" became a
byword for judicial and para-judicial abuse in fairly short order.
It would be more than a century and a half before the court was
abolished by the Long Parliament in 1641.

111   See "Keeping Quiet: The downside to 'voluntary laicization'" by
Christopher R. Altieri in *The Catholic Herald*, 11 December 2020.

112   See "Crime & Punishment: Church leaders' disastrous refusal
to abandon secrecy" by Christopher R. Altieri in *The Catholic
Herald*, 3 June 2021.

113   In fact, the ample quote from which the maxim comes is even
more instructive, as are the particulars of the case that occasioned

it, along with the biographical details of the remark's author, Gordon Hewart, 1ˢᵗ Viscount Hewart, Lord Chief Justice of England from 8 March 1922–12 October 1940. The case was <u>Rex</u> *v*. <u>Sussex Justices</u> (1924), a bench trial of a personal injury claim resulting from a motorcycle accident. When both sides had rested, the deputy clerk of the trial court retired with the judges, who deliberated and then delivered a judgment against the defendant. The deputy clerk, however, just happened to be a partner in the law firm representing the plaintiffs. So, the defendant appealed.

The trial judges swore unanimously that the deputy clerk— actually the acting deputy clerk on the day, brother to the deputy clerk—took no part in their deliberations. In fact, no actual impropriety on the part of the judges or the deputy clerk (or anyone else) was ever alleged. "It is said, and, no doubt, truly, that when that gentleman [the deputy clerk] retired in the usual way with the justices, taking with him the notes of the evidence in case the justices might desire to consult him," Lord Hewart in his judgment wrote, "the justices came to a conclusion without consulting him, and that he scrupulously abstained from referring to the case in any way." That was not Lord Hewart's last word. "But while that is so," he wrote, "a long line of cases shows that it is not merely of some importance but is of fundamental importance that justice should not only be done, but should manifestly and undoubtedly be seen to be done."

"Nothing is to be done," Hewart wrote elsewhere in his judgment, "which creates even a suspicion that there has been an improper interference with the course of justice."

114 As the great twentieth-century political philosopher, Eric Voegelin, put it in his work on *The New Science of Politics: An Introduction* in 1954:

> [U]nder the title of political societies in form for action, the clearly distinguishable power units in history come into view. Political societies, in order to be in form for action, must have an internal structure that will enable some of its members— the ruler, the government, the prince, the sovereign, the magistrate, etc., according to the varying terminology of the ages—to find habitual obedience for their acts of command;

and these acts must serve the existential necessities of a
society, such as the defence of the realm and administration
of justice—if a medieval classification of purposes will be
allowed. Such societies with their internal organization for
action, however, do not exist as cosmic fixtures from eternity
but grow in history; this process in which human beings
form themselves into a society for action shall be called the
articulation of a society. As the result of political articulation
we find human beings, the rulers, who can act for the society,
men whose acts are not imputed to their own persons but
to the society as a whole—with the consequence that, for
instance, the pronunciation of a general rule regulating an
area of human life will not be understood as an exercise in
moral philosophy but will be experienced by the members of
the society as the declaration of a rule with obligatory force
for themselves. When his acts are effectively imputed in this
manner, a person is the representative of a society.

Though it is far beyond the scope of this book, it is interesting
to consider that the Catholic Church is a representative institution—all institutions somehow are representative—in the
threefold Voegelinian sense. Societies have elements of representation, which are the organs of power; those organs must
secure habitual obedience and meet the needs of the people,
those providing what Voegelin calls "existential" representation
or representation of existence; societies exist in an idea of order,
representing to the membership the truth about the way things
are, how the universe hangs together, what is justice, etc.

115 Cf. Montesquieu, *De l'esprit des lois*, Paris: 1748, *passim*. This
author's go-to copy is the English translation of Montesquieu's
monumental work that is part of the Cambridge Texts in the
History of Political Thought, published in 1989. There are several
versions in both the original French and in English, many of
which are freely available online.